National Extens

CW00743266

HOW TO
STUDY
EFFECTIVELY

The secret of success

Carol A. Harman
Richard Freeman

NATIONAL EXTENSION COLLEGE

If you are buying *How to Study Effectively* on its own you can still enrol as a correspondence student and enjoy the guidance of an experienced tutor. For details write to the National Extension College, 18 Brooklands Avenue, Cambridge CB2 2HN explaining that you have already purchased the book.

The National Extension College, 18 Brooklands Avenue, Cambridge CB2 2NH

© National Extension College Trust Ltd. 1972, 1984
ISBN 0 86082 446 2

The National Extension College is an adult teaching body providing education through correspondence courses, publishing, tapes, slides and kits, weekend study sessions and day seminars. As a non-profit making company, registered as a charity, all monies received by NEC are used to extend and improve the range of services provided.

National Extension College correspondence units are a range of self-tuition texts designed for use by adult students. These texts are suitable both for use by home based and college based students. Colleges interested in materials for class use should write to the Executive Director for a catalogue of materials available.

First edition 1972
New edition prepared by Carol Harman 1984
Cartoons by Steve Way
Set in 9 point Palatino by Cambridge Photosetting Services
Printed by the National Extension College, Cambridge 1984

Reprinted 1985
Reprinted 1986 with corrections
Design: Cover   David Cutting Graphics
            Text   Peter Hall
Photographs: John Walmsley

ACKNOWLEDGEMENTS
pp. 36–42   Article by W. Perry is taken from Harvard Education Review, vol. 29, 1959.
            Copyright © by President and Fellows of Harvard College.
p. 45   Entry 705 from Roget's *Thesaurus*, edited by Sue Lloyd, is reproduced by
            permission of Longman.
pp. 57–62   Articles © Times Newspapers Ltd.
p. 80   Articles © The Observer Ltd.
p. 82   The passage from *Letter to a Teacher* is reproduced by permission of Penguin Books
            Ltd. The book is translated by Nora Rossi and Tom Cole.
            © School of Barbiana, 1969. Translation
            © Random House, Inc., 1970

HOW TO STUDY EFFECTIVELY

CONTENTS

ASSIGNMENTS

TUITION IN STUDY SKILLS

If you are aiming to work through this book on your own, why not take advantage of NEC's distance-learning course in effective studying?

On enrolling with NEC you will be given an experienced correspondence tutor who will guide you through *How to Study Effectively*, providing you with personal guidance and commenting on three of the student assignments (A, C and E).

You will also be given three computer-marked assignment forms, enabling you to obtain rapid feedback on assignments B, D and F using MAIL, NEC's computer-managed marking system.

How to Study Effectively is of course invaluable however you choose to work through it. But if you would like to enrol on the NEC course, and enjoy the full benefit of NEC's wide experience in teaching study skills, send for an enrolment form and further details to:

FREEPOST, NEC, Cambridge CB2 1BR

INTRODUCTION

1. THE PURPOSE OF THE COURSE

This course is intended basically for *independent* students who:

- are following or intending to follow a correspondence course
- want to do private study at home
- are following a radio or television course.

The course should also be useful to students at universities and colleges – similar courses at American and British universities have proved to be very successful.

There is good chance that you haven't studied recently. Indeed, you may not have been very successful at school, and this may be the reason for your coming back to study as an independent student. Thus you may feel uncertain of your ability to take up a course of study. This course can help rid you of that fear. You can learn how to study, whether or not you once did well at school. *Learning efficiently isn't a gift that you were born with. It is a skill which you can be taught to develop.* This course will explain how you can develop that skill. By careful study of this course and through working on all the activities and assignments, you will steadily teach yourself to study effectively. Of course, you are not going to reach your peak learning power at the end of this short course; but you should have a clear appreciation of the ingredients of successful learning. You will know what techniques to practise and what to avoid. Gradually, if you follow the instructions in this course, your confidence in your ability to learn will increase.

Almost certainly, you have more commitments than a full-time student at university or college. You may have a job, a family to look after or other responsibilities. It is people like you who need, more than anyone else, to learn to study *efficiently*. This course will help you to make good use of the time you have, so that when you are studying you are also learning.

Activity 1: Motives

One of the reasons why students don't pass their courses is that their motivation is not strong enough.

You should begin by working out in your own mind your own special reasons for studying.

1. *Answer the following questions in the box below as honestly as you can:*
   - *Why did you become a student?*
   - *Why did you start this particular course?*
   - *How is the course going to help you?*
   - *Why do you want to complete it?*

My reasons for taking this course:

2. *Now put* G *next to all good reasons and* B *next to the bad reasons. For example,*

   if $G = 8$ *and* $B = 4$ *then,* $\left(\dfrac{G}{G + B}\right) = \dfrac{8}{12}$ $\left(\dfrac{8}{12} \times \dfrac{100}{1}\right) = 66.6\%.$

   If your score is low (e.g. below 60%) you will have to rethink about starting to study. When the subject becomes boring and you feel like giving up, look again at the good reasons.

2. PLAN OF THE COURSE

This is a course – not a textbook – so you will find frequent suggestions for work to be done. It is important that you do this work at some stage of the course, even if not at the first reading. One way of working through the course is as follows. Set aside 1½ to 2 hours and read right through the course. Ignore all the work suggestions and the pieces you don't understand at first reading. Then leave the course alone for at least a day. Then come back and work through Unit 1 slowly, following the guidance contained in the course.

There is no fixed period of time for the course. In Unit 1 Section 2.1, you will be asked to make your own overall plan.

3. USING THE COURSE WITH OTHER STUDIES

How to study effectively is designed to help you develop good study habits. You will be able to practise these skills if you are taking another course at the same time, though ideally you should work through Unit 1 of this course before you start the other course. You will need the skills developed in Units 2–5 throughout your other course, so you should refer to each skill as you need it. You will not need Unit 6 until about six weeks before your examinations.

4. WORKSHEETS AND YOUR TUTOR

In addition to the activities for self-assessment on this course, there are three assignments to return to your tutor for guidance and comment. Most correspondence students hesitate about sending in their first worksheet because they think their tutor wants a 'perfect' answer. What your tutor really wants is to help you, and he or she can only do so if you send him some work. If you find difficulty in completing your first worksheet, send your tutor part of it so he can help you finish the rest. Your tutor is an expert long-distance teacher. Please make full use of him/her. Although you may feel shy about doing so, it is a good idea to write a letter to your tutor to introduce yourself. You could tell him/her where you live, where you work, your hobbies and interests, and any special factors that affect your study plans. This will help to build up a personal relationship and give your tutor a better understanding of your work.

5. COMPLAINTS AND DIFFICULTIES

We've tried to make this course fit the needs of students returning to learning. But with your help we can make it even better. At the end of the course there is a blank page for your comments. Please use this if you would like to tell us what you think about the course. If you are having difficulties, either with the content of the course or your method of study, write or ring straightaway. Your tutor is paid to help you and is always willing to do so.

6. THE AUTHORS

Richard Freeman is Director of NEC. A former teacher, he became interested in helping students through four years work as the Head of the Advisory Service at the Advisory Centre for Education (ACE).

Carol Harman is a Lecturer in Education at Mitchell College, Bathurst, New South Wales, Australia, where she teaches a study skills course. She has also spent five months researching study skills courses in the United Kingdom. Most of this time was spent at the National Extension College.

4

UNIT 1

WHEN & WHERE TO STUDY

In studies, whatsoever a man commandeth upon himself, let him set hours for it.

BACON

1. OBJECTIVES

When you have worked through this unit and carried out the related activities you should be able to:

- work out a study plan showing how you are going to complete this course
- say precisely how you spend your time at the moment
- say which hours on which days you are going to use for studying
- work out the best surroundings for you to study effectively, and get the equipment that you will need.

2. PLANS AND TIMETABLES

Successful students invariably have well-designed plans and timetables. (They may not have them written down, but almost certainly they have a plan in their heads.) A plan is an overall view of the course of study and will usually cover a term or a year. A timetable is a more detailed day-to-day division of time and covers not only study but, to some extent, the other activities which are essential to your life.

Timetables are great aids to efficiency. Firstly they enable you to analyse the use you are making of your time. Is it the most effective scheme? Are the hours allocated to study the best ones? A timetable also takes a load off your mind. Just as listing pressing commitments (*see* Unit 2, Section 2) enables you to concentrate on the one task in hand, so timetabling the day's or week's routine ensures that all the decisions have been taken in advance. Without a timetable you will have to make a hundred decisions each week as you try to fit everything in. The very making of the decisions will tax your energy and leave you less ready for study.

2.1 The overall plan

To conduct this plan you will need:

- a clear overview of the course
  (One way of doing this is to set aside 1½ to 2 hours to read right through the course, looking carefully at the headings for each unit and noting the number of activities and assignments.)
- a realistic appraisal of all your present commitments.

Activity 2: The overall plan

1. *Buy or make yourself a wall calendar showing the months during which you intend to do this course.*

2. *Block out the time you will not be able to devote to study,*
   e.g. family holidays
   weekends away
   when you are likely to be very busy at work and will have to stay late, or bring work home
   school holidays – if these are a busy time for you.

3. *Mark on the calendar*

- *the times you will not be able to devote to study*
- *the time you plan to spend reading and doing the activities for each unit*
- *the time you are going to spend on each assignment – plan for more than you need just in case it takes longer than you think.*

It is also a wise precaution to plan these tasks for early in the week, particularly if your lifestyle is unpredictable, and other demands are likely to be made on your time.

A typical month may look like this:

February

					Weekend	
1	2	3	4	5	6	7
Away		Read & do activities for Unit 1				
8	9	10	11	12	13	14
			my			
	Write		birthday		Assignment 1	
15	16	17	18	19	20	21
		Check Assignment 1			Post assignment	
22	23	24	25	26	27	28

If you are studying more than one course you can use a code (e.g. different coloured pens) to write out your plan for each course.

Planning your work in this way has the following advantages:

- You ensure that you put in work regularly.
- You don't panic because you have left your work until the last minute.
- Once you have completed the work that you planned for a particular number of days, the rest of the days are free from the worry of not getting your work done.
- By allowing a span of days rather than one day to do your work, you can then cope with unforeseen interruptions.

2.2 The weekly timetable

Now that you have decided on your overall plan of work each week, you need to work out exactly *when* you are going to do it. Many of your weekly activities are already fixed for you by your family, your social group, or by your employer (if you are working). As a part-time student you will need to fit in your study periods around these other commitments. This involves:

- looking in a detailed way at how you use your time
- deciding which times you will be able to study.

Activity 3: How do you use your time?

Using the timetable on page 9, fill in how you used your time last week. If you can't remember, try keeping a record for this week. (You will need to make a record once or twice a day, otherwise you may not remember.) You do not need to be absolutely precise. The aim of this activity is for you to find out what time you generally have free from other commitments, and could use for study each week. Don't forget to count lunch hours, time spent travelling on public transport, time when your children are asleep. In fact, any time when you have not got a set commitment. Mark these times on your timetable with S (for study).

This is not to suggest that you use all these times for study. You need to eat and have fun as well! The aim of this exercise is just to let you see what times are usually free. Treat these periods in a flexible way by:

- *deciding on your study goal for the week and using as many of these study periods as you need to achieve this goal.*
- *experimenting with different study times, e.g. early in the morning, early in the evening, late at night. This will help you to find out at what times you work best. Different people work best at different times. Don't worry if you have difficulty at one time – try another.*
- *reward yourself by doing things you enjoy in the other periods, e.g. watching television, reading a book, going to the pub.*

Many people motivate themselves to study by deciding on a goal for a particular day (or evening) and promising themselves a reward when they have finished. This really helps you to get started, and not to become easily distracted. Most people find it very hard to study, so do not worry if it is difficult for you. The great Italian dramatist, Alfieri, even made his servant tie him to the study table!

---

3. HOW MUCH TIME FOR STUDY?

The amount of time you need for study depends quite simply on the amount of study you need to do. Start off with four hours a week and then adjust your schedule as you go along. You will find that some tasks take longer than you think – others take less time. You may be a slow reader, but comprehend well. The extra time spent in reading means that you may need less time for the asssignment.

One method of handling this is to:

- write down the study tasks you plan to do during a week
- decide early in the week when you are going to do these tasks.

Weekly Timetable

Time	Monday	Tuesday	Wednesday	Thursday	Friday	Saturday	Sunday

Usual waking time ← Write in 1 hour intervals → Usual sleeping time

A typical list may look like this:

Study tasks – week beginning 7 March	
1. Read Unit 3 Course A.	On the train Monday
2. Do the four activities in this unit, Course A.	7–9 p.m. Tuesday
3. Read three chapters for Course B.	Lunch hour Wednesday
4. Make notes on these chapters in preparation for Assignment 4.	7–8 a.m. Thursday
Extra times in case of unforeseen interruptions: lunch hour Thursday & Friday, and Thursday evening.	

Cross out each task as it is completed. This will give you a feeling of achievement.

Helpful hints:

- Use short periods of time for reading the text.
- Keep longer periods (e.g. 2 hours) for assignments.

Activity 4: A weekly plan
Using the example given as a guide, write out your study tasks for next week.

---

4. WHERE TO STUDY

People with a busy lifestyle need to be adaptable. You won't always be at home when you have time to study. You may be at work or you may be travelling to work. In fact one can safely say, 'You can read your study books anywhere that you can read the newspaper' – for some people this includes the bath! However, when you are taking notes or writing out assignments, you need a more suitable environment. For this purpose you need a set place to work. Some people will be fortunate enough to have a special room for study. Others will have a study-bedroom, a seldom-used dining-room, or some other part of the house which is as free as possible from distractions. Two vital aids to this sort of study are:

- a writing surface (a desk or table);
- a space to put your books, notes etc. where they can be organised, and where you can safely leave them until you return to study.

Try enlisting the help of your family.

You could make some simple shelves with planks and bricks for this purpose:

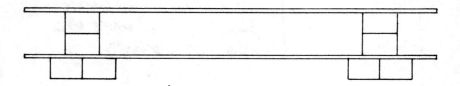

A display board can also prove invaluable for charts, timetables and diagrams. You can make a very simple one by buying a sheet of pin-up board from a hardware store and either screwing it to a wall or resting it on your desk/table. It helps to keep material in front of you without cluttering your desk.

N.B. It is very important for you to organise your material well, so that you don't lose pieces of paper and spend a lot of time hunting for a particular book. You could have special places on your shelves for different items, and keep your work in well-labelled folders. More hints on filing will be given later in this course.

ASSIGNMENT A

Please do this assignment and send your work to your tutor at the end of your work on Unit 1. Don't worry about trying to write 'perfect' answers! The assignments are mainly to give your tutor the chance to try to help you with any problems you may have.

Please answer ONE of the following questions; write one or two pages (200–400 words or so).

1. Make a list of the things that tend to get in the way of studying for you personally. Then, for each problem, try to decide on a method you might use to overcome it. Comment on any particular difficulties you have where you can't think of a way round the problems concerned (and your tutor will try to help).

OR

2. Describe your approach to timetabling studying, both on a week-to-week basis, and on an hour-to-hour basis. What do you find are the best times for your studies? How have you found out what works best for you personally? Describe briefly any further things you might do to experiment with ways of making your studies even more efficient.

OR

3. Describe the place you study in, and how you have organised it so that your studies are efficient. Describe also any ways in which you think you may be able to use *other* places to fit in some *further* studying from time to time.

UNIT 2

LEARNING EFFICIENTLY

Continuity of thought upon one single thing, and the suppression of every source of distraction, multiply in an extraordinary way the value of time.

ALFIERI

1. OBJECTIVES

When you have worked through this unit and carried out the related activities you should be able to:

- fix your attention and interest on the topic being studied
- list your reasons for wanting to study
- work out techniques for understanding new information
- understand how your memory works
- practise some aids to memorising
- decide how to promote discussion about the course
- write down a list of good study habits for yourself

2. ATTENTION AND INTEREST

If you are going to learn efficiently, you must concentrate your attention on the subject to be studied. All the time your brain is receiving ever-changing stimuli – noises, movements, messages from your body (hunger, cold, being uncomfortable etc.) and you pay attention to each in turn. Normally you only attend to any one stimulus for a few seconds.

Now when you want to study, you are choosing to pay attention to one thing – the piece of work to be studied – so you should start by ridding yourself of unwanted stimuli. Some are easy to remove, simply by the right choice of where and when to study (*see* Unit 1). Others are more difficult. For example, you can easily get away from the distraction of other members of the family by choosing a different room. But what if you are worrying about one member of the family? To eliminate this sort of distraction is more difficult. Try, for a start, to avoid coming to study after some other excitement such as an argument or a discussion. The quieter your mind, the easier it will be to attend to your studies.

You may also have a lot of other things to attend to. They won't get done simply by worrying about them when you are studying. The best way to deal with them is by making a list or a timetable, which you should have set out in Unit 1. Your work timetable settles, in a general way, when you are going to study. Having decided this, note down when you are going to do the other things still on your mind.

For example:

Shopping	*Pay*
Coffee	Gas (by 26/5/84)
Potatoes	
Bread	
Biscuits	*Ring*
	Christine
Write to	
Mum & Dad	

Keep a note-pad on your desk for this purpose. As each task is completed cross it off, and when the majority of the tasks are done start a new list including tasks that are still outstanding.

This simple listing or timetabling should satisfy you that everything can be done in the time available. If you *do* find that you have too much to do in too short a time, you should decide on which tasks are priorities and allocate a definite time for doing the rest. Then your mind will clear and will be ready to concentrate on studying. However, even when you have cleared your mind and settled down to study, other thoughts will attract your attention from time to time. You must try and suppress these and a useful method is to work at a fair speed. Since attention can only be maintained on any one point for a few seconds, attempting to concentrate too long on one point invariably invites a stray thought to grab your attention. By working faster you keep switching your attention from one point to another, but in this case all the points are relevant to your studies.

Interest naturally leads to attention. No-one will make a good job of studying what doesn't interest him. You can maintain interest in various ways. Firstly, use lots of sources of ideas and information. This helps to give you plenty of viewpoints on a subject and keeps your interest aroused. Secondly, try to relate the subject all the time to everyday life and in particular to your own life. This approach is particularly successful if your studies are related to your job.

Of course, there will be times when it is essential to master a particular point in which you just can't rouse any interest. Don't evade these points. Tackle them head-on by reserving one of your best study times for an onslaught.

Attention and interest summary

- Remove irrelevant and unwanted stimuli, e.g. noise, hunger, cold.
- Put aside other pressing matters by listing or timetabling them.
- Suppress unwanted thoughts by quickly switching to the topic under study.
- Understand what you are studying.
- Take a lively interest in the subject outside your study hours.

Activity 5: Increasing attention and interest

Write down what you have done to put this section into practice.

- *How did you 'clear the decks' for study?*
- *How will you relate what you are studying to your everyday life? (e.g. How will you make the best use of your time at work/home?)*

3. MOTIVATION AND GOALS

Successful students not only have good study habits and techniques, but they are highly motivated. They want to study.

There are many different reasons for wanting to study. Universities have always placed great emphasis on learning for learning's sake: for them, being interested in the subject is sufficient motivation. But most of us have a more mundane motive for study. Quite often the reason is to get a better job. Never spurn this motive. It is one of the most powerful drives for keeping you at your studies. If you are studying for a vocational reason, try to keep this in your mind. Think about how your studies will relate to your job and career in the future.

Activity 6: Motivation

1. *Place a tick in the box if the statement applies to you. My studies will help me:*

   get a more fulfilling job ☐
   get more pay ☐
   get a chance to move to a better town ☐
   feel more self-confident ☐
   play a greater part in the community ☐
   impress my children ☐

2. *Now write down other factors that motivate you:*

This activity may have helped you to see the kinds of motivation that keep you going. But your vocational motive is a long-term aim – the reason for embarking on and sticking to your course. You will also need short-term goals to keep you going week by week, day by day. For each and every study session you should set yourself definite and realistic goals. Definite in the sense that you will be able to feel at the end of the session whether or not the goal has been reached, e.g. mastering one chapter of a book. Realistic in the sense that you are aiming neither too high nor too low. Too low a goal will give you no satisfaction in achieving it; too high a goal will deprive you of the satisfaction of reaching it.

Repeated experiments have shown that students are most successful when they have a clear knowledge of their progress. You should get into the habit of checking on your progress. For example, having completed work on a chapter, quickly note down from memory the main points. Then compare them with the original. Note your strengths and weaknesses and resolve to make up those weaknesses at the next study session.

Good motivation is always tied up with interest in the subject. There are many ways of livening up an area of study. Try reading a book on its history. Try to find out how your subject relates to other subjects. Find out how it comes into everyday life. Look out for films, and television and radio programmes connected with the subject. All these approaches will stimulate your interest and increase your motivation.

Motivation summary

- Keep your vocational aim in mind.
- Have clear and realistic goals for every study session.
- Check your progress at every session.
- Read around your subject.

---

4. MEMORY

Most students would agree that one of their main difficulties is remembering what they have learnt. It is widely believed that (1) each of us possesses a faculty called 'memory' and that (2) some of us have better memories than others. It is also widely held that (3) practice in memorising poems or chunks of the Bible helps to develop our memories. All these beliefs are erroneous. A person who is good at memorising material for examinations is a person with good study habits. Nor is knowledge a matter of deliberately memorising lots of material. Knowledgeable people keep notes and use reference books for most of the information that they need. It is only important to remember key points. This will ensure that you have some 'pegs' to help you recall information when you need it (e.g. for examinations). Some 'memory tricks' will be given later in this unit.

It is helpful to understand a little about how learning takes place and how memory works.

The important points to remember are:

- Understanding and reconstructing material are crucial to remembering it.
- Learning does not take place at a steady rate.
- You have a long-term memory and a short-term memory.
- Mnemonics (aids to memory) are useful for remembering key points.

4.1 Understanding and reconstructing material

If you were asked to memorise a line of Greek or a mathematical formula, and knew no Greek or were not a mathematician, you would have to memorise every twist and turn of the pen on the paper. But a Greek linguist or a mathematician would quickly learn the word or formula. They would not do so because they have better memories than you. Their success is solely due to the fact that the line of Greek means something to the linguist and the mathematical formula means something to the mathematician. They memorise the material easily because they understand it. So if you are having trouble understanding new material, try each of the following steps in turn. (Step 5 is only a last resort!)

1. Make sure you understand all the words. If they are unfamiliar, look them up in a dictionary.
2. Try substituting familiar words for unfamiliar ones.
3. Leave the section for a while and then come back to it with a fresh mind.
4. Ask a friend.
5. Ring or write to your tutor.

Once you have understood the material you then need to remember it. Your memory works like a filing system. You have to know where to look for information before you can find it. Most psychologists believe that our memories do not get worse as we get older, but that older people have many more memories to search through for the information they need. It is therefore important to 'file' information in your memory so that facts are linked to each other in a logical way. This involves:

- linking new material with what you have already learned
- taking good notes (this will be dealt with in Unit 4)
- summarising all notes so that the key points are highlighted
- making connections between the various components – in practice this might involve making charts, diagrams, tables etc.

Activity 7: Linking what you have learned

Turn to an informative article in a newspaper or magazine. List the main points that are being made. Then, by the side of your first list, write down some of your own examples of the points being made. For example:

Courteous Driving

Point	Example
Indicate well in advance your intention to turn right or left.	*When I am driving into my own home.*
Make sure you are in the correct lane.	*When I am on the motorway.*
Indicate apppreciation when someone allows you to move into their traffic lane.	*When I am on the motorway.*

4.2 Learning does not take place at a steady rate

Most subjects are too complex to work out the precise rate at which learning occurs. But analogies can be made from graphs of learning physical skills such as typewriting. In the following graph, or 'learning curve', the number of typewriting strokes that can be made per minute is plotted against the amount of practice.

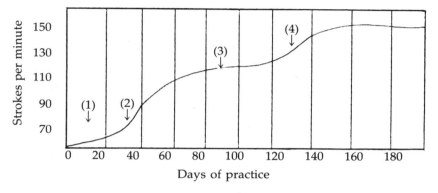

Fig. 1: Learning curve for typewriting

At stage (1), little progress is made because the subject is unfamiliar to the student. Then he enters stage (2) and makes rapid progress. After stage (2), during which he learnt quite a lot of material, he enters stage (3) – the plateau. Here he seems to be in the doldrums. Despite effort, no progress seems possible. This plateau is a dangerous place, since it is here that the student may feel defeated. Making little progress, he loses confidence and throws in the sponge. The plateau is the particular enemy of the home student who fails to realise that everyone reaches this sort of stage. But if only he perseveres, he eventually moves on to stage (4) when once again progress is rapid, as in stage (2). At the end of stage (4), the student reaches his peak in this particular topic.

4.3 You have a short-term memory and a long-term memory

4.3.1 Short-term memory (up to twenty seconds)

This can hold a few facts for a short time, e.g. the first half of a sentence while you are reading the second half. The way your short-term memory works can be illustrated by the following activity.

Activity 8: Short-term memory

1. *Turn to a telephone directory and pick out a number at random. Read it through once and try to remember it. Then without looking at the directory write it down. Can you remember it?*

2. *You probably answered 'yes'. Now find another number at random. Read it through. Don't write it down or run through it in your mind. Do something else for five minutes. Can you remember it this time?*

You probably answered 'no'.

There are two things to note about short-term memory:

- It only holds information for a short time. If you do nothing to reiterate the information you will forget it.
- It can easily be overlooked. Try doing Activity 8 with two numbers. It is much more difficult to remember all the digits. (Seven is the magic number most often quoted for short-term memory.)

4.3.2 Long-term memory

Once you have taken material in through your short-term memory, you will often wish to transfer it to your long-term memory. As we have already pointed out, your first step is to understand the material. Then you must link the new material to what you have already learnt. This process is called making 'chains of association'. The following activity will help to explain this.

Activity 9: Making chains of association

Pick a set time from yesterday evening (e.g. the time you arrived home, or the children came in from school). Picture that event in your mind: where it happened, who was there, what they were doing. Then gradually build up a picture of the sequence of events which took place. If your memory falters, concentrate on the preceding event and try to remember more and more details. If you write this down, more and more things will come into mind as you write. If something springs to mind out of sequence, just jot it down. Your mind will get taken up with other things and that particular fact may not come back. (This is good advice for exams too.) If you have 'linked' your study material, the chains of association will help you recall information.

4.4 Mnemonics (aids to memory)

At times you may have to resort to some 'memory tricks' to help you remember key points. People who specialise in this are the sort of people who enter contests like 'Mastermind'. A few examples of memory tricks are given below. If you would like to master more of them, a reading list is given at the back of this book.

- One method is to remember a sentence in which the first letter of each word is also a letter of each item on the list you want to remember. For example, all the names of the notes on the treble clef are: e g b d f. Your mnemonic could be 'every good boy deserves fruit'.
- Another method is to make a word out of the first letter of each word on your list. This may be a nonsense word, e.g. ana-as-ae. These are the first letters of the seven continents – Africa, North America, Antarctica, Asia, South America, Australia, Europe.
- Rhymes can also be a useful method for remembering facts, for example:

> In fourteen hundred and ninety-two,
> Columbus sailed the ocean blue.

If you find it difficult to use these techniques, write the items you need to remember on a small piece of paper and carry it around in your pocket. Each time you look at the paper you will remember more items.

Activity 10: Mnemonics
Make a list of the items you need to memorise by rote. Work out some mnemonics to help you remember them. Your list of items should, of course, be short. When dealing with longer strings of ideas, it is much better to understand them and use your 'chains of association' to recall the facts.

Memory and learning summary
- Never try to memorise what you don't understand.
- Always try to link new material with what you have already learnt.
- Select the most important items to learn.
- Organise selected items.
- Place your material in a logical sequence, with connections between each component.
- Use mnemonics when learning by heart.

5. USE OF DISCUSSION TO PROMOTE LEARNING
So far all the techniques have been relevant to individual study. That is not surprising since learning is an individual process. A group can *study* together but they *learn* as individuals. Now we come to a very important method of group activity which promotes individual learning and understanding – discussion.

Section 3 emphasised the need for a clear knowledge of your progress.

Students who check their progress at regular intervals learn faster than those who plod on with no checks on what they have learnt. But isolated students – at home, say – may find it difficult to check their progress. They think they understand something which in reality they are still confused about. Discussion avoids this problem. You try explaining something you've just learnt to someone else. You're doing fine – and then they ask a question. Suddenly you don't know. You realise that, after all, you hadn't mastered the topic. Don't despair. You've just learnt something very important. You've learnt that you don't know something, or don't understand something which previously you felt sure of. You have a clearer picture of your own progress. Through the discussion you have discovered which points you need to concentrate on in your next study session.

Discussion will also give you new ideas and new insights through listening to someone else's ideas and experience. In fact the discussion process combines several functions.

- Discussion tests your knowledge and understanding.
- Discussion brings you new ideas and insights.
- Discussion is an active reordering of the material in your mind.

You should, therefore, take every opportunity to discuss your subject with other people. They don't have to be experts, although experts should by no means be avoided. But you can learn by talking over your subject with friends and family even when they have never studied the subject. Indeed, Mao Tse Tung is reputed to have said that the educator's job is to give the people in a clear and organised form what he has learnt from them in an unorganised form. So do try to tap your friends for ideas.

Activity 11: Using discussion to promote learning
1. *Next time you are talking to a friend ask them how they remember:*

- *telephone numbers*
- *their spouse's birthday*
- *important events at work and/or home.*

2. *Then ask them how they remembered facts when they were at school.*

6. DEVELOPING LEARNING HABITS
'Successful studying, like successful dieting, calls not for sporadic bursts of good behaviour but for long-term adjustment to the pattern of one's daily habits.'

(The Open University *Study guide* 1970, p. 6)

Unless you have no need of this course, you should already be aware of discrepancies between good study habits and your own habits. How can you make the change?

Habits – good or bad – are, by definition, deeply rooted. They are not changed easily. If you wish to study effectively, you must be prepared to make a clean and determined break with all old habits which hamper effective study. This will not be easy.

Activity 12: Learning habits

First, list all the habits and activities that are hindering your study. Include distracting activities like watching too much television. Then list all the good habits that you need to develop. Then resolve to make a clean break with the first list and rigorously follow the second list.

Sticking to your new behaviour is very difficult at first. But stick to it you must, if you wish this behaviour to become a habit. There are various ways of reinforcing the new behaviour. *Try enlisting the help of your family.* Tell them of your new intentions and ask them to remind you of any lapses. You can understand the effectiveness of this approach by considering the repentant smoker. A personal decision to give up smoking is hard to keep. Who will notice if you have 'just one more'? But, if you tell all your friends and family of your intention to stop smoking, every reach for a cigarette will be greeted with a chorus of reminders of your intentions. So it is with study habits. Use your family or friends as your conscience until the new behaviour pattern is an established routine – a habit.

You can read your study books anywhere that you can read the newspaper.

ASSIGNMENT B

This is a MAIL test, and will be marked by a computer at NEC, so please send it directly there and not to your tutor. Fill in a MAIL answer form with the letter corresponding to the option you choose for each of the questions.

1. You've just started this assignment (don't stop now!); tell me how much time elapsed between *deciding* to do this assignment now, and making your first mark on the assignment form:
   A less than 5 minutes.
   B between 5 and 20 minutes.
   C I decided to do it yesterday and here I am doing it today!
   D you don't really want me to confess, do you?

2. Why did you start this course? Which of the following fits you best?
   A I was tired of being in a rut and decided to do something about it.
   B I need to get some qualifications, and want to make sure that I'll be successful.
   C I hit serious study problems in the past, and want to avoid them in future.
   D I enjoy studying anyway, and want to enjoy it even more by making it more efficient.

3. How well do timetables for studying work for you?
   A I enjoy making them, but I don't stick to them.
   B Timetables have revolutionised my efficiency, thanks!
   C I find it hard to estimate how long a task will take.
   D Timetables are not for me. I'm more efficient with my own method of making sure my studying gets done.

4. What's the ideal place for you to study? Choose the option that suits you best.
   A A quiet room, free from interruptions, not too warm, not too cool; with a good big table or desk.
   B A corner of a busy room with other people present and quite a few distractions.
   C I'm alright, I've got a proper study already.
   D I don't mind really; I work in all sorts of places (though not with maximum efficiency in each place!).

5. Are you a 'morning person'? Have you *tried* studying in the early morning? Which of the following answers is nearest yours?
   A No, it's no use me trying to study in the morning.
   B Yes, I find I study well first thing in the morning.
   C I work better at night, so I'm not going to start studying in the mornings as well.
   D I've got too many things to do already at the start of the day; I can't fit studying in as well.

6. Suppose you needed to learn a definition, but it didn't make any sense to you. What would you do?

   A Learn it anyway, and hope that after a while you'd start to understand it.

   B Go back and try to understand what the definition was about, then learn it.

   C Skip that definition, no point learning something that doesn't make sense!

   D Make a note of the definition and look for clues about its meaning elsewhere, maybe asking for guidance from a tutor.

7. Which do you think is most important when learning a subject?

   A Trying to get a working knowledge of all the material concerned.

   B Selecting the most important parts and learning these really well.

   C Doing a lot of reading around the subject.

   D Trying to spot likely exam questions, and practising your answers to them.

8. You've just had 'flu, and are a week behind in your studies. What would you do?

   A Plan a 'solid' day in which to catch up, then continue on schedule.

   B Plan to spend an extra half-hour or so a day catching up over the next week or two, in addition to your normal study schedule.

   C Decide to continue as normal, but a week late.

   D None of these. Having flu and being off work meant that I did quite a lot of extra study, and I'm ahead of schedule.

9. This question is to help us discover what you think of the course so far. Which of the following fits you best?

   A I've learned many useful things already.

   B I knew most of this already, but I still think it's useful.

   C I'm not convinced. I'll have to try out a few things before I can tell whether they're useful or not.

   D I'm afraid there are lots of things in the course that are no use to me.

10. This question is to find out how useful you found the *previous* assignment, and your tutor's comments. Pick the statement closest to your feelings.

    A My tutor's comments were extremely helpful, thanks.

    B My tutor's comments were quite helpful.

    C My tutor didn't seem all that interested in my views or my problems.

    D I didn't actually send my tutor that assignment.

UNIT 3

READING

There is an art of reading, as well as an art of thinking, and an art of writing.

ISAAC D'ISRAELI

1. OBJECTIVES

When you have worked through this unit and carried out the related activities you should be able to:

- decide what to read for your study purposes
- distinguish between the various types of reading, decide when each is appropriate, practise their use
- check your reading speed and adjust speed to purpose in reading
- increase your vocabulary
- practise the SQ3R method of studying a book
- use your books more effectively.

2. READING

Reading is the most important single skill in study, but no single publication will provide you with all the information you need. Students have to make two important decisions:

- What to read
- How to read in the most effective way.

2.1 What to read

Successful students do not learn only from text books. They also read novels, periodicals, reference books and newspapers. But they try and ensure that these are as relevant as possible to their studies.

To find out quickly whether or not a publication is relevant and likely to be useful, check:

- The title. Does it relate to the topic you are studying?
- The preface/foreword/introduction. This will tell you the purpose of the publication.
- The author. Is he/she a recognised authority on the subject? If you have not heard of him/her before, is there a section in the book which tells you the author's credentials?
- The date of publication. If you are studying in a field which changes rapidly and the book is over ten years old, check in your library to see if there is some more recent work on the topic.
- The place of publication. If you are studying in a field where different nations approach the topic differently, try to find a book from your own country.
- Has your lecturer or tutor mentioned the publication? Was the reference favourable?
- The footnotes and bibliography:
  Is the bibliography comprehensive?
  Does the author refer to recent publications?

2.2 How to read in the most effective way

Skilled readers vary their reading speed and method to suit both the material they are reading and their purpose in reading it.

If you are looking through a list of exam results to find your own result, you scan the list very quickly for your name. Having found your name, you will read the result against it very carefully – you'll probably read it several times just to make sure that you haven't made a mistake. This illustrates very clearly how you can vary your type of reading according to your purpose: scanning for some vital point (your name); detailed, slow attention to extract the crucial detail (your result).

As a student determined to study effectively and efficiently, you should try to cultivate this varied approach to reading. Here are some of the types of reading which you will need.

3. TYPES OF READING

3.1 Skimming

Skimming is a quick and efficient way of familiarising yourself with a publication. When some people pick up a book – to take some notes, for example – they plunge straight in at the beginning and work steadily through to the end. This is a very time-consuming process and a very inefficient way of finding information. If you want to find information or ideas quickly in a book what you should do is look at:

- the table of contents (this will list the chapter headings and may also include sub-headings)
- the index
- sub-headings in the text
- chapter summaries (if there are any)
- first and last paragraphs (or sections) of chapters; first and last sentences of paragraphs
- figures and diagrams

In a periodical, you should look at:

- the summary at the beginning (if there is one)
- the sub-headings
- the first and last paragraphs (the latter usually contains the conclusions)
- figures and diagrams

After skimming material in this way you have three choices:

- Decide the book/periodical is not suitable.
- Decide that certain sections are appropriate to your needs.

- Decide that you need to read all of it. Even in this case your skimming has still been useful as it has given you an overall view of the material.

So you benefit whatever your reaction.

Activity 13: Skimming
Using the steps explained on p. 31, skim this book.

3.2 Scanning

Scanning is a very rapid search for some important point. It may be a page number, a title or a key word. The essential thing is that you deliberately ignore everything except the one item for which you are scanning. Some people are very bad at this because they don't try hard enough to concentrate. They let their attention wander and start reading interesting (but irrelevant!) paragraphs, until they entirely forget their original purpose.

Good students need to become good scanners. They may have to scan books or notes for a point to include in an essay, or they may have to scan periodicals and indexes for subjects which are important to their studies. Bad scanners allow their attention to be caught by matters which are only incidental to the matter in hand. If you find that your scanning is poor, turn back to Unit 2 Section 2 and try to apply the advice of that section to your scanning.

Activity 14: Scanning
Give yourself three minutes to find out the following information about this book.

- *Are bibliographies mentioned in the table of contents?*
- *On what page does the sub-heading 'Short-term memory' appear?*
- *How many times is the word 'skim' mentioned in the section on skimming?*
- *Is there a book on memory techniques in the 'Further reading' section?*

3.3 Reading to study

This is perhaps the type of reading which we normally associate with study. It is slow and repetitive. The aim is to master what is being read. At the end of reading one chapter in this way, you will hope to have absorbed all the major facts, ideas and arguments in that chapter. Reading to study may well involve several readings and the taking of notes to summarise what has been read. Reading to study is dealt with in detail in Section 6.

3.4 Light reading

This is the way most of us read most of the time. Many novels and newspapers are read like this. But obviously, not all novels and newspaper articles are suitable for such treatment. For example, Tolstoy and Forster, *The Times* and the *Guardian* deserve far more studious treatment. They put forward ideas of great moment and they demand that you study, criticise and assess those ideas.

3.5 Word by word reading

There are certain types of material that demand word by word reading. They only need to be mentioned so that you don't feel ashamed when you find that you need this technique. The two most important areas in which word by word reading is required are foreign languages and mathematical and scientific formulae.

The ability to 'read' a line of print depends on familiarity with the material. Readers automatically recognise common words and phrases without actually focussing their eyes on every word and letter. Thus you only need to glance at

a stitch in time saves nine

to know what it says, whereas a word like

methoxyhaemoglobinaemia

takes a lot of looking at. Yet 'methoxyhaemoglobinaemia' contains only one more letter than 'a stitch in time saves nine'.

Thus the eye has to stop and dissect unfamiliar words, whereas it can take in familiar phrases at a glance. Since most foreign words are unfamiliar to a new student of the language, a word by word reading will be needed before words and phrases become familiar.

Mathematical and scientific formulae are much like a foreign language, except in one respect. Formulae are highly condensed methods of conveying information. The simple formula H_2O contains the statement 'the substance which is formed when two atoms of hydrogen are combined with one atom of oxygen'. Without formulae, scientists and mathematicians would be buried under words. You must, therefore, expect to greatly slow down your reading whenever you read a formula. Of course, familiarity with a subject leads to familiarity with basic formulae patterns. Thus

$$x = \frac{-b \pm \sqrt{b^2 - 4ac}}{2a}$$

is instantly recognised by all mathematicians, but for the school student it represents quite a feat of understanding!

Activity 15: Choosing a reading method

Which of the five methods of reading would you choose for the following?

1. *Looking at a book in a shop and deciding whether to buy it.*
2. *Reading a novel.*
3. *Looking up the meaning of a word in a dictionary.*
4. *Reading the instructions for assembling a model.*
5. *Finding the meaning of dyslexia in a book on reading problems.*
6. *Studying for a history exam from a text book.*

Your answers will vary since there can be several equally valid ways of approaching any reading task. My answers would be:

1. Skimming, with possibly some scanning.
2. Light reading.
3. Scanning (to find entry) followed by reading carefully, word by word.
4. Word by word.
5. Scanning (to find entry) followed by reading to study or word by word.
6. Reading to study.

Types of reading summary

To study efficiently you must learn to vary your reading speed to suit both the material in front of you and your reason for reading that material. You must first aim at mastering each type of reading in your studies and, if speed is important to you, in leisure reading. By developing the ability to switch from one method of reading to another, you will vastly increase your efficiency. You will be able to search for specific items by scanning, to assess a passage quickly by skimming, to analyse and master a passage by studious reading. Nor should your lighter reading be neglected. Here, too, you can increase your efficiency by learning to read light or familiar material at a much faster speed than your present reading. The next section discusses ways of improving your reading skills.

Activity 16: How you read now

1. *List all the things you remember reading in the last three days (don't forget to include newspapers, advertisements etc.).*
2. *Now put 1, 2, 3, 4, or 5 against each item according to the reading method you used when you first read each item. Did you always use the most appropriate method? If not, you should try to do so in your further reading.*

Develop the ability to switch from one method of reading to another.

4. READING SPEED

Students who cannot keep up with the reading material set for their courses often blame their slow reading speed. They have developed the habit of reading each piece of material from beginning to end, and even when the lecturer says, 'You don't have to recall all of this book, just take a quick look at it', they feel that they cannot possibly understand the ideas properly unless they read the entire book. These students are not adapting their reading to their purpose. In contrast, efficient students decide which of the five types of reading they should use to get the information they need.

The following exercise will show whether you read for a purpose.

Activity 17: Reading for a purpose

1. *Allow yourself two minutes to study the extract printed below.*

2. *Write down what you think it is about.*

3. *Take fifteen more minutes and see if you can extract any more information.*

4. *Compare 1 and 3. Did you get the main points in the first two minutes?*

Students' use and misuse of reading skills

Mr President, twenty years ago this Faculty undertook an experiment to see if some of its students could be taught to read better. Since the Faculty was then something of a pioneer in such an enterprise, it would seem appropriate that it should receive, after two decades, at least a report of progress – the more so because the work now concerns not the correction of disabilities of a few students but the direction of the abilities of a large proportion of the freshman class.

The students of this college are reputed to spend a good deal of time reading. In fact, a student sits with his books for nearly a thousand hours each year. The Faculty has a deep concern that these hours be fruitful. This concern is evident in the wording of assignments, in the layout of instruction in each course, and in the conversations of teachers with their students. It was this same concern that started the original experiment in reading improvements in 1938. The experiment began with a rather mechanical emphasis. It consisted of an instructor, whose main job was to run a projector for the first Harvard Reading Films, and some thirty student volunteers, hopefully the worst readers in the freshman class (and at that time there apparently were some freshmen who for Harvard's intents and purposes found it hard to read at all). The class met for about 18 to 20 sessions and engendered enough enthusiasm to become, like many an experiment, a kind of annual fixture, this one known as the Remedial Reading Course. Each year freshmen as they arrived in the fall would take a reading test and those who scored lowest would be informed of their plight and allowed to volunteer for the continued experiment.

When the Bureau of Study Counsel took over the actual instruction in this course in 1946, we met with thirty depressed-looking volunteers one evening in a basement class-room somewhere. Not knowing really what we were up against, we gave them still another reading test of a standard sort and discovered that every single one of them could score better on this test than 85% of the college freshmen in the country. We felt that to be useful to these people in their genuine dissatisfaction we were going to have to take a new look at the reading improvement game. We therefore abandoned the word 'Remedial' for the course and upgraded the material until it could jar the teeth of the average graduate student. Then we threw the doors open.

The amount of enthusiasm that exists in this community to read better – or if not better, then at least faster – is evidenced by the fact that we soon found ourselves with nearly 800 people enrolled in the course. When we examined the roll, we found that we had some 400 freshmen from Harvard and Radcliffe, 100 upperclassmen, 230 graduate students from the various schools, especially that of Business Administration, and two professors – from the Law School.

Although the fees paid by these multitudes looked very attractive on the budget of a small office, we came to feel this was stretching our energies too far. We have subsequently cut the class in half and have been trying to make some sensible system of priorities whereby we might offer first chance on seats to roughly that third of the freshman class that might be most likely to benefit from this kind of instruction. In trying to find out who these people might be, we have turned up some observations about freshmen which may be of interest to the Faculty.

One wonders first of all why students who read, on tests, as well as these do, should want to attend a reading course at all, much less one that meets daily at 8 o'clock in the morning. Of course a number come in hope of magic – some machine they've heard of that will stretch their eyes until they can see a whole page at a glance. This is understandable. Freshmen are deprived rather abruptly of the luxury of thinking that reading is something they can finish, and are confronted instead with an infinite world of books in which they sense that they may forever feel behind, or even illiterate.

But year by year it has become more apparent that what the students lack is not mechanical skills but flexibility and purpose in the use of them – the capacity to adjust themselves to a variety of reading materials and purposes that exist on a college level.

What they seem to do with almost any kind of reading is to open the book and read from word to word, having in advance abandoned all responsibility in regard to the purpose of the reading to those who had made the assignment. They complain consequently of difficulty in concentrating and feel that they have 'read' whole assignments but are unable to remember anything in them. We have therefore shifted the emphasis of the reading course away from mechanics over to an effort to shake students loose from this conscientious but meaningless approach to their work. We have found that if they can be persuaded of their right to think, even though reading, they can then develop a broader and more flexible attack on the different forms of study and put their skills to meaningful use even on long assignments.

In offering freshmen priority on seats in the course, therefore, we have naturally wanted to know about their flexibility and their sense of purpose in reading. This is a hard thing to measure. To make some estimate of it we designed a new kind of reading test – as reading tests go it may really be rather peculiar – and presented it to the freshmen of Harvard and Radcliffe when they arrived this September. We suspected the students might learn more from it than we would, but this seemed a legitimate chance to take. I should like to describe this test and to tell you what the students did with it.

First of all, instead of the usual short passages which appear on reading tests, we presented students with thirty pages of detailed material – a complete chapter from a history book. We asked them to imagine they were enrolled in a course entitled The Growth of Western Institutions. We asked them to picture themselves sitting down of an evening to study one assignment in this course – this chapter entitled 'The Development of the English State, 1066–1272'. They were to suppose that they had two hours ahead of them for this work, but that after all, they still had their French to do and some Chemistry to review before they went to bed. At the same time, they were to imagine that in this course an hour-examination would be given in about a week on which they would be asked to write a short essay and to 'identify' important details. We told them to go ahead about their reading in whatever way they thought best and to take notes if they wished. We told them this was a test of what they derived from the early stages of their study of regular assignments and that in about 20 minutes or so we would stop them and ask them questions appropriate to their particular method of work. We then turned them loose.

Twenty-two minutes later we stopped them and asked them what they had been doing. If they reported that they had been reading from the very beginning and going straight ahead into the chapter – whether rapidly the first reading, or carefully with a more rapid review in mind – we gave them regular multiple-choice questions on the chapter as far as they had gone in it. Up to this point the test was fairly standard, and we can report that the vast majority of the students, over ninety per cent of them in fact, reported that this was exactly what they had done. We can report that their rate of work in this particular approach was astonishing and their capacity to answer multiple-choice questions in detail was impressive. Some of them had read as many as twenty pages of very detailed material and were able to answer accurately every sensible question we could ask them about the detail.

The freshman class – as far as we could see – of both Harvard and Radcliffe, consisted of a most remarkable collection of readers – in the narrow sense of the term. The showing is most remarkable because, of course, these ninety per cent of the class were going at this chapter in the hardest way imaginable.

Let me explain what I mean. The chapter in question is an admirable piece of exposition, but like many admirable chapters it makes no initial statement of its aims, and it takes a little while to get going. And as a consequence, the reader who begins at the beginning with the Battle of Hastings and reads word by word is likely to find himself at page three hopelessly bogged down in the shires, the hundreds and the marches of Anglo-Saxon England. And after ten minutes or so, this was just where the students reported themselves to be. What we were interested to determine was how many students in the face of this burden of detail, the purpose of which was not clear, would have the moral courage – or should we call it the immoral courage – to pull themselves out and look at the end of the chapter. Or even to survey the entire marginal gloss set out like sign posts page by page. The very ending has a bold flag out beside it which says – 'Recapitulation'. As a summary paragraph we doubt that we have ever seen a better one. From a half minute of study of this paragraph the whole development of the chapter becomes immediately clear to a reader and puts him in a strong position, not only to select among details as he reads them, but also to remember, for their meaningfulness, the details he would need to support an intelligent discourse.

Out of these 1500 of the finest freshmen readers in the country only 150 even made a claim to have taken a look ahead during twenty minutes of struggle with the chapter. And the vast majority of these seemed to have looked ahead only to determine how long the assignment was.

We asked anyone who could do so to write a short statement about what the chapter was all about. The number who were able to tell us in terms that had something to do with the growth of institutions, was just one in a hundred-fifteen.

As a demonstration of obedient purposelessness in the reading of 99% of freshmen we found this impressive. We had been looking for the one-third of the class most in need of our beneficent instruction and we had found just about everybody. We tried to find out if the students had behaved this way simply because it was a test – they reported no, that they always worked this way. When we pointed the ending out to them, some said, 'You mean you can sometimes tell what a chapter is about by looking at the end' and others said, 'O Lord, how many times have I been told!'

Told or not, after twelve years of reading homework assignments in school they had all settled into the habit of leaving the point of it all to someone else. We knew from our own efforts to reach independence of approach in reading that students find it hard to hear us even when the sheer bulk of college work could be handled in no other way. And we supposed that school-teachers had an even harder time of it. We were therefore prepared to find this widespread passivity of purpose; we wished to go beyond this and to identify those students whose misconceptions of reading involved something worse, a positive misconception of aim, a notion of the purpose of reading so at variance with the goals of Harvard that they might be especially slow at learning from their college experience. We had therefore added another turn to our test.

We asked students to imagine further that in their imaginary course an examination had been given on which an essay question had appeared.

This question (which we hoped was a proper-type Harvard essay question) reads: 'From 1066–1272, the Norman and Angevin Kings laid the foundations of English self-government both by their strengths and by their weaknesses'. Discuss. (Twenty minutes). We then presented them with two answers, purporting to have been written by two students. The first of these was a chronological reiteration of the chapter by a student with an extraordinary memory for dates and kings and no concern for the question (or for any intellectual issue at all, for that matter). We calculated that no instructor with a shred of compassion in him could give this answer less than a C— even though it might deserve less. The second essay answer, shorter, and with hardly a date in it, addressed itself stringently to the issues posed by the question. We supposed this answer to be worth a B+, or perhaps an A— to a relieved instructor.

In validating the test, we had then begged the assistance of the chief section man in a real course, not wholly unlike this imaginary course of ours, and asked him to grade the essays. Of the first, he said that he really couldn't give the student a D because he had worked so hard; of the second we were pleased to hear him say that this was obviously an A student, even though all he was going to get on this essay was a B+.

To the freshmen, then, we presented on the test these two answers without reporting their value and asked them to state which of the essays was the better, which the worse, and to give their reasons. We are happy to say that on this they did quite well. Only two hundred students graded the better essay the worse, and only two hundred more gave the wrong reasons for the correct grading. This means that, on this particular measure, only a rough third of our freshmen showed themselves to be headed toward the wrong goals. Very possibly, were this same test to be given later in the year, the percentage would be much less. But we have experience to support that the tendency persists – often tragically.

These then were the students to whom we turned our attention. Until such students revise their sense of the purpose of reading, an increase in effort is likely to produce only worse results. Oddly, we have as yet found nothing else to distinguish them from other people. The number of them who come from public schools as against private schools is exactly the same as for the class as a whole, and they are by no means the least intelligent members of their class. We are eager to find if we can learn more about how they get their misconceptions. We hope that the Reading Course may help to turn some of them around. Perhaps the test itself helped; the section man who helped us with the test was quick to point out its instructional possibilities, and we gave the text and essays to the students to take with them, together with a page of comments. It was encouraging to have to thread one's way afterwards through knots of students working over their papers.

What might the Faculty conclude from all this? As the Faculty's agent in this area, I can report my own conclusions from this twenty-year experiment.

1. It appears that most students can learn to read better.
2. The instruction that assists them to do so does not center in the mechanics of reading. The mechanics of reading skill are inseparable

at this level from the individual's purpose as he reads. If you train someone in mechanics alone, he drops right back into his old habits the minute he picks up an assigned text.

3. The possession of excellent reading skills as evidenced on conventional reading tests is no guarantee that a student knows how to read long assignments meaningfully. The fact that the Admission Committee is providing students of higher and higher ability should not lull the Faculty into feeling that at last it does not have to teach students how to study. In fact the responsibility is only the greater, for these students have the ability to muddle through assignments the wrong way and still get that wretched C—.

4. There can be no general rules for teaching the exercise of judgement in reading. Such judgement requires courage, and courage cannot be taught by rule, it can only be dared, or redirected, in ways appropriate to particular subjects and learning tasks. To be sure, the reading of conflicting authorities is a fertile ground for young courage, and an excellent exercise in reading skill. And a C— for the attainment of useless knowledge is perhaps less of a kindness in the long run than congratulations for effort and a clean E for expending it in the wrong game. However, the individual instructor in his own course remains the best judge of how to set up his assignments so that they demand a redirection of effort towards effort and away from ritual.

5. A short separate course of general instruction, like the Reading Class can be of some contributing value, if only because if offers a moment's freedom to experiment without the threat of failure. But its limits are very clear. In such a course we can only dramatize the issues, and this only in the area of very general expository reading. We can refer only briefly to science and must leave literature explicitly alone.

We feel, too, that only a narrow line of spirit divides such instruction from an invitation to mere gamesmanship. We sometimes worry, in teaching method without content, lest students gather that we recommend a glance at the ending of chapters and at nothing else. (We do dare students to suppose that even this is sometimes appropriate.)

I should like to be able to report, in conclusion, that when we do succeed in introducing students to the rigors of thoughtful reading they are invariably grateful. I must confess, a bit ruefully, that this is not always the case. I have here a description of this kind of instruction in a student's words. To assist us in developing the course we have occasionally given the students a questionnaire at the end, and this one of a year or so ago was a real up-to-date Social-Science-type questionnaire: open-ended at the beginning, pointed at the end, and all. It says here, 'What did you expect when you came to this course?' Big space. 'What do you think about it now?' Big space. On the other side a lot of specific questions. We did not ask students to sign their names, only to enter the scores they made at the beginning and end of the course.

This student's scores when he came to the course showed him to have derived only a D— kind of understanding from considerable study of the material. At the end he was obtaining a straight A understanding in one-third of the time. I remember settling back with this one in anticipation of those comments that a teacher so loves to hear – but not at all. He was furious. 'What did you expect when you came to this course?' 'I expected an organised effort to improve my reading.' 'What do you think of it now?' 'This has been the sloppiest and most disorganised course I have ever taken. Of course, I have made some progress, but this was due entirely to my own efforts . . .'

From: Perry, W. Students' use and misuse of reading skills, *Harvard Educational Review*, vol. 29, 1959. Copyright © President and Fellows of Harvard College, 1959.

4.1 How fast do you read?

There are many exercises which can be used to increase reading speed (*see* the Further reading list for some of these). However, it is very difficult to get a *reliable* indication of the speed at which you read. If the material is familiar, if the vocabulary is simple, and/or if you are interested, you tend to read faster. And beware of speed-reading teachers who simplify the material in order to produce good results in their pupils:

'I took a speed-reading course, learning to read straight down the middle of the page, and I was able to go through *War and peace* in 20 minutes. It's about Russia.' – Woody Allen. (Quoted in *Psychology Today*, August 1972.)

If you wish to get a rough indication of your reading speed try the following activity.

Activity 18: Reading speed

1. *Find a passage of familiar material (that used for Activity 17 would be suitable).*

2. *Count the number of words it contains (Activity 17 has approximately 3,360 words).*

3. *Calculate your speed of reading in words per minute as follows:*

$$\frac{length\ in\ words \times 60}{time\ in\ seconds} = words\ per\ minute$$

If your reading speed is below 200 w.p.m. then you need to practise reading faster by reading short passages as quickly as you can. Keep a record of your speeds on a form like this:

Reading speed

Test no.	Date	What read	Length in words	Time in seconds	w.p.m.

Be careful to choose material of similar difficulty, e.g. the same newspaper each day. Otherwise your speed may vary because of the varying difficulty of the material.

The following points will help all readers to improve their speed:

- Decide on your purpose before you start.
- Apply this purpose to your reading by concentrating on the main ideas.
- Always skim new material first.
- Scan for key words.
- Train your eyes to see more in each eye movement. Instead of moving them along each line of print concentrate on the centre of each line.
- Do not look back after you have read a difficult sentence. Keep going and see if the meaning becomes clearer. If necessary, go back when you have finished the section.
- Avoid mouthing the words. The way to overcome this is to read faster than you can speak.
- Increase your vocabulary (*see* the following section).

5. EXTENDING YOUR VOCABULARY

When it comes to study, one of the commonest difficulties is lack of familiarity with the language used by the authors you read. The normal vocabulary of everyday gossip is limited to 2,000–3,000 words. The average person has a latent (i.e. total words he knows, whether or not he uses them) vocabulary of 20,000–25,000 words, whereas his active vocabulary is nearer the 3,000-word gossip level. But for study, a minimum latent vocabulary of 25,000 words is needed. To feel completely at home in study, a level of nearer 40,000 words is needed. How can you bridge the gap?

Extending your vocabulary is quite easy and is nothing like learning the lists of words which teachers used to be so fond of. The lists of difficult words printed in popular magazines do not, as claimed, improve your vocabulary. The mere learning of words and their meanings quickly fades from memory, and as fast as you take in new words you are losing words learnt two to three weeks ago. No, successful vocabulary building relies on applying our knowledge of memory and learning (*see* Unit 2, Section 4). You will remember that material which is understood, is linked with previous knowledge and is applied in everyday life, is mastered and memorised more quickly than material which is learnt by rote. The following guides to a better vocabulary are all based on this simple principle.

5.1 Read widely

Almost all the words you know were learnt in context. That is, as a child, you heard others use the words over and over again in many different contexts, and so you learnt the meaning of the word. Any other method of learning would be impossibly complex for a child. Imagine trying to define 'pretty' to a five-year old! Yet most five-year olds use the word without the slightest difficulty. They do this because they have an intuitive understanding of what 'pretty' means from the various occasions on which it has been used by others.

Similarly, the best way in which adults can broaden their vocabulary is by reading widely so as to meet new words in a variety of contexts. It is, of course, no use just doing a lot of reading in one field. A diet of novels or biology or horror stories will not do. You would not meet enough new words in a sufficient range of contexts to clearly establish them in your own vocabulary.

5.2 Use new words

Some new words will find their way into your vocabulary without any conscious effort. But you can also gain something by deliberately using new words as you meet them. It may help to list those words which you feel are of particular importance – e.g. those which you will need for your studies. You can then look at the list and determine to use some of the words in the near future.

5.3 Looking up words

On the whole, we learn very few words through consulting dictionaries. But occasionally you will meet a word without being able to grasp its meaning from the context. When this happens, look up the word in a dictionary and make a note of its meaning. You can go over such lists from time to time, but don't try to commit them verbatim to memory. You may find it useful to have Roget's *Thesaurus* to hand. This book has been continuously in print since 1852, which is measure enough of its value, and a major revision of the text has been undertaken for the latest, 1982 edition. Words are grouped under topics.

e.g. Entry 705 in the Penguin edition is 'opponent' The entry reads:

705. Opponent – N. *opponent*, opposer, lion in the path; adversary, antagonist 881 n. *enemy*; assailant 712 n. *attacker*; the opposition, ranks of Tuscany, opposite camp; oppositionist, radical; obstructionist, filibuster 702 n. *hinderer*; crossbenches; die-hard, irreconcilable; radical of the right, reactionary; objector 489 n. *dissentient*; non-cooperator 829 n. *malcontent*; agitator 738 n. *revolter*; challenger, other candidate, rival, emulator, competitor; entrant, the field, all comers 716 n. *contender*.

All the words are listed in an alphabetical index to the Thesaurus which quickly guides you to words and phrases suitable to a particular context. The Penguin edition of the *Thesaurus* is very good value for money. If you prefer a hardback edition, but don't want to pay a lot, look in second-hand bookshops.

5.4 Other techniques
There are also several painless ways of extending your vocabulary – for example, games like 'Scrabble' or completing a daily crossword puzzle.

Activity 19: using your dictionary
1. *Find words in today's newspaper which you do not understand.*

2. *Find out their meanings in a dictionary.*

3. *Write each word on a separate slip of paper and write out the meanings on a piece of scrap paper.*

4. *Produce the words several times during the course of your evening's study and try to write down their meanings correctly each time. Use your original jotting as a check.*

6. SQ3R
This is not a mathematical formula nor a mysterious code. SQ3R simply stands for:

S	Survey
Q	Question
R	Read
R	Recall
R	Review

It is a useful method of approaching a passage, such as a chapter of a book, which you want to study and master. The idea is that your reading of the passage is broken down into five stages. The details of each stage are explained below:

6.1 Survey

This is rather like the skimming process which you met in Section 3. To survey a book you look at the following items:

- title
  author
  date of first publication and date of this edition.

And then:

- read preface and introduction
  look at contents page
  look at the bibliography as a means of checking the range of research and to provide suggestions for further reading
  read chapter headings
  familiarise yourself with the index.

The *survey* stage gives you a general impression of the type of book you are reading. If you are going to concentrate on one chapter, the *survey* stage ensures that you also have an adequate impression of the book as a whole. The date of publication ensures that you have an idea of the historical context in which the book was written. Obviously you will approach a book on chemistry written in 1850 or even 1950 in a very different way from a chemistry book of 1980.

Reading the preface and introduction ensures that you understand the author's intention in writing the book. He may explain why he has taken a particular line, why he has omitted certain items and so on.

Looking at the index is a guide to the type of notes you might wish to make. A poorly indexed book, or one with no index at all, requires better note-taking than a well-indexed book.

6.2 Question

Before embarking on the book or chapter, ask yourself what you expect to gain from the book. Why are you reading the book? What points are you particularly interested in? These sorts of question ensure that you read with a purpose.

You might even ask, 'Is the book worth reading?' To answer this, read its first and last paragraphs, then its first and last chapters. This should help you decide whether it's worth studying.

6.3 Read

You will find it best to read a chapter at least twice at a fair speed before you study it in detail. You will be looking for the author's general stance for this chapter and also for the basic idea in each paragraph. Then you will look at the detail. What evidence does the author produce to back up his argument? Look at his examples, his proofs. Can you think of any contrary examples? Is there a flaw in his proof?

Look at the diagrams and illustrations. What purpose does the author have in choosing these diagrams and illustrations? What points do they illustrate?

Then look at the author's case in the round. Is the chapter convincing? Are there alternative theories which would do just as well in the circumstances? What consequences flow from the author's theory? What consequences flow from your alternative theories?

You will notice that at the beginning of the *read* stage, you are simply trying to grasp what the author says. You are trying to understand his arguments. Only when you completely follow the author's case do you turn to criticising it. If you criticise too soon, you will fail to listen to what the author has to say and be carried away by your own ideas.

6.4 Recall
This stage may follow the *read* stage for the whole chapter, or, if the chapter is rather lengthy or complex, it may follow the *read* stage for sections of the chapter.

The *recall* stage involves trying to recall all the main ideas in the section under recall. It is best either to recite them aloud or to write them down in note form.

6.5 Review
The *review* stage is the checking which follows recall. Look back over the chapter and check that your recall was correct. Make a special note of any important points which you failed to recall, or which you wrongly recalled.

Activity 20: SQ3R
Take a chapter of a book you are studying, or any book which is of interest to you. Apply the SQ3R technique to the chapter as follows:

1. *Survey*
   (a) *the book itself using the headings on p. 46.*
   (b) *the chapter by looking at the headings, sub-headings (if any), first and last paragraphs, figures and diagrams (if any).*

2. *Question. Write down the questions you hope to be able to answer by reading the chapter.*

3. *Read.*

4. *Recall. Jot down the answers to your questions.*

5. *Review what you have jotted down by referring*
   (a) *back to your questions*
   (b) *to the chapter itself.*

At the end of the activity you should have a good understanding of the chapter. SQ3R is a powerful method. Try to use it regularly.

7. CHOOSING BOOKS

If you are following a set course of study, there will almost certainly be some books which are compulsory reading. In addition to these, there will probably be a list of recommended books. It is very unlikely that you will have time to study more than a small section from the list, so you must choose the books with care.

It is usually best to delay buying any but the set books until the course is under way: until you begin to get the feel of the subject you will not be able to make an informed choice. If possible you should ask other students for their recommendations, which may be just as valuable as those of lecturers.

The sort of books which you will need to buy are:
- Compulsory texts
- Reference books
- Dictionary
- Thesaurus
- Books which are referred to often throughout the course.

You will also need some books for short periods (e.g. for a particular assignment). Whether you buy these books or borrow from a library is you own decision, but whatever you decide you will need to plan well ahead. Bookshops often do not stock the books you need, and will have to order them for you. Similarly, library books you want to borrow will often be on loan, and to avoid this you will have to book well in advance. You may sometimes have to try two or three libraries for particular texts.

8. YOUR OWN LIBRARY

Ideally, you should aim to build up a small collection of books in your subject. This can be a very expensive process, so be on the look-out for book sales and secondhand bookshops, and ex-students wishing to sell their books. Although books *are* expensive, bear in mind that your collection will save you many trips to libraries and your books will be constantly available when you need to refer to them.

As your library grows you will find it useful to catalogue your own books in some logical way. You will get ideas on how to do this in the next chapter.

ASSIGNMENT C

Please complete this assignment, and send it to your tutor at the end of Unit 3.

Please answer TWO questions. Each answer should be about 200–400 words.

1. Choose a book that seems relevant to you (maybe to your studies, or to your work – or even to a hobby or interest of yours).
   (a) Try out the steps under the sub-heading 'What to read' at the start of Unit 3, and write down your reactions as you apply these steps to the book of your choice.
   (b) Skim the book, following the list of suggestions given under 'Skimming'. As you go, make notes about how useful (or otherwise) you regard the information you derive from the book while skimming. You might write a few lines on each of the following (and other ideas of your own):
   - table of contents
   - index
   - sub-headings in the text
   - chapter summaries (if present)
   - first and last sections of chapters
   - figures, tables, diagrams
   - any other features of the book that prove useful to you as you skim.

2. Apply the SQ3R method to a newspaper article (pick a fairly long one – about a page or so). Send your tutor the following:
   - the questions you write
   - the notes you make
   - the article itself (so your tutor can see how you have got on).

3. Write brief notes about various aspects of your reading habits, including:
   - the sort of material you read for pleasure
   - 'more serious' reading material
   - how you adapt your reading technique to match the purpose of your reading
   - any reading problems you have now solved
   - any remaining reading difficulties.

▶

4. Describe the sort of reading material that you expect to deal with in your future studies. Decide how best you might approach your task of reading to study, in relation to the sort of material you expect to be studying.

UNIT 4

NOTE-TAKING AND FILING

The palest ink is better than the most retentive memory.

CHINESE PROVERB

1. OBJECTIVES

When you have worked through this unit and carried out the related activities, you will be able to:

- understand the purpose of note-taking
- examine and analyse your existing notes
- list the characteristics of effective notes
- make effective notes
- explain when and where you can best use sequential and nuclear notes
- explain the purposes of filing
- discuss different filing systems
- decide on the best way of filing your study material.

2. NOTE-TAKING

2.1 The purpose of notes

(a) To aid memory

The primary purpose of notes is to aid memory. You can't hope to retain a whole lecture, book or discussion permanently in your memory, so instead you make notes of the most important items and use the notes for revision and reference. The items you select for inclusion in the notes should be sufficiently detailed to enable you to reconstruct the rest of the material.

(b) Reordering and reorganising study material

We have already stressed the importance of reordering and reorganising study material (*see* Unit 2, Section 4). The making of notes is one of the most useful opportunities for rearranging material in whichever form is most convenient to you. This function of notes is *not* served by the printed notes sold by booksellers. You might as well memorise the original lecture or book, as memorise printed notes!

(c) Aiding concentration and promoting learning

Making notes on a particular passage requires more concentration and effort than does plain reading. Active study, such as recitation and writing, promotes learning and holds the concentration far better than passive study, such as reading. For instance, many children cannot learn to read simply through using printed readers and cards. Instead, they have to feel the shape of letters and words by cutting them out of sandpaper or tracing them in sand. These methods are just as useful to adults; you will find the use of physical activity in the form of note-taking essential to efficient study.

Of course, the overall purpose of making notes is to gain success in your studies. It is helpful to bear this in mind when deciding what to include in your notes and how to arrange them: notes which do not help towards this long term aim should be discarded.

Activity 21: Looking at your notes

1. Look back over one set of study material and find the notes you made.

2. Ask yourself the following questions:

- *Can I read these notes?*
- *What are they about?*
- *Why did I make them?*
- *Did they serve that purpose adequately?*
- *Reflect – how good are my note-taking skills?*

2.2 Characteristics of good notes

There are no hard and fast rules here, simply because notes are such a personal learning aid. On the whole, though, the following general observations apply to most types of notes.

Notes should be brief and clear. If they are too long, you will find it tedious to wade through them, either to look for a specific point, or to refresh your memory.

Once made, your notes are your primary source of information and, if you are to take an exam, you will be aiming at complete familiarity with their contents. So at the outset, you should create notes which you can understand. If you cannot quickly read through them to refresh your memory, they will fail in their purpose.

Activity 22: Checking your note-taking skills

For each of the sets of notes you used in Activity 21, tick which of the following characteristics they had:

Easily read	☐	*Difficult to read*	☐
Brief	☐	*Long*	☐
Clear	☐	*Unclear*	☐
Easily understood	☐	*Difficult to understand*	☐
Organised the way I learn	☐	*Organised in some other way*	☐
Relevant to my needs	☐	*Not relevant to my needs*	☐

Have you given yourself lots of ticks in the left-hand column? If you have, then your note-taking system is already excellent. But if you have lots of ticks in the right-hand column, then you need a new approach to note-taking.

2.3 Notes from books

When taking notes from books remember the following:

(a) Evaluate the books (*see* Unit 3)

(b) Write down:
- title
- author
- publisher
- place of publication
- date of publication.

If it is from a library, also write down the classification number (printed at the base of the spine) for future reference.

(c) Use the skimming technique to see which parts of the book are most relevant (*see* Unit 3).

(d) Use the SQ3R technique (*see* Unit 3, Section 6) to find out the main points in the chapters.

(e) Make notes in your own words. The process of converting the ideas into your own language also ensures that you understand the material. In making permanent notes you will want to do your own rearranging of the material, and possibly you will want to add your own comments and cross-references to other notes.

(f) Record the main topics and then note the important points under each topic. These will tend to be headings or brief statements. Where an argument, proof or sequence of reasoning is presented, try to note down the main steps, but don't pare the argument down so much that you can't restate the missing processes.

(g) You should also record the major conclusions or results of each chapter. Thus your framework might be something like this:
- Chapter heading (in your own words, maybe).
- Important points.
- Illustrations and arguments to support points.
- Result/conclusions.

Of course, you shouldn't regard this as a skeleton outline for all note-taking, but it does illustrate the type of organisation you should be aiming at when making notes.

(h) Record the page numbers of the sections you are noting. For instance 'Brown – 27' means that the notes came from p. 27 of Brown's book. In this way you can recheck a point subsequently if you need to. Always remember to put quotation marks around material which you copy exactly from a book. You can then use your quotation (with an appropriate acknowledgement) in your essay without having to return to the original page to check details. This can save you a lot of time.

2.4 Notes from lectures

In order to make the best use of any lecture you attend:

(a) Be familiar with the topic. Read as much as you can in advance. This will make the lecture easier to understand and help you to recognize the main points.

(b) Sit where you can see and hear the lecturer.

(c) Note:
  • the subject of the lecture
  • the lecturer's name
  • the date.

(d) Try to work out the plan of the lecture. To what extent you can make usable notes at the time depends on the competence of the speaker. Some ramble on, back-track or lose their way, until no-one knows exactly what stage has been reached. With such a lecturer, it may be impossible to write down topic headings during the lecture. This unfortunately means that the student has a lot of extra work to do afterwards. Where this is the case, go over your notes as soon as possible after the lecture, before the detail fades from memory. If your notes are still confused, talk about them to another student. This may help to clarify them.

If you find that two or three of you are confused, go to see the lecturer concerned. You may be embarrassed about doing this, but your study is too important to be ignored. Provided you are reasonably courteous, this strategy often results in the lecturer agreeing to put headings on the chalkboard or use transparencies to clarify important points.

(e) Ask questions during and/or after the lecture if you do not understand every point.

(f) Remember that the lecturer is usually the person who sets the exam. Watch for the points that he/she emphasises and read the material that is recommended to you.

2.5 Layout of notes

The type of notes you take depends upon your purpose in taking them. If you are writing an essay, then you should use a card system which is flexible (*see* Unit 5 on Essay writing).

If you are taking notes for general use (e.g. for seminars and/or revision), then you can use:

Sit where you can see and hear the lecturer.

2.5.1 Sequential notes

These are continuous notes and involve highlighting by headings and then subdividing material (see below for an example).

When taking these notes remember to:

(a) Use headings and subheadings.

(b) Number these to differentiate between points.

(c) Emphasise material by for example:
- underlining
- using different colours
- using capital letters.

(d) Use abbreviations. But be careful that you are consistent and can remember what the abbreviations mean.

2.5.2 Nuclear notes

This method is described by Tony Buzan in his book *Use your head* (BBC Publications, 1974). With this method:

(a) you write the main topic in the centre of the page

(b) you then write related ideas around it and link them up to show their relationship to the main idea

(c) you can also add links around the edges to show relationships.

Buzan claims that his method is not only quicker to write and read, but because the notes reflect the relationships between ideas, they create chains of association (*see* Unit 2) and therefore aid memory.

Activity 23: Sequential and nuclear notes

1. *Read the passage 'How divers' bones die 1,000 feet under' (below) and then look at both the sequential and nuclear notes given (pp. 59–60). Which set do you prefer? Why?*

2. *Read the passage 'Why dentists go on practising after deaths of patients'. Write your own*
   (a) sequential notes
   (b) nuclear notes
   Which set do you prefer? Why?

How divers' bones die 1,000 feet under

One of the true terrors of the deep for North Sea divers is a painful, insidious and potentially crippling condition known as aseptic bone necrosis – literally the death of bone. According to a major report published this month, bone necrosis among divers is on the increase. A survey of the medical records of 5,000 commercial divers by researchers at

---

Newcastle University shows that the number of men suffering from the disease is increasing steadily as the search for oil moves into deeper and deeper water.

"The fact is, the deeper you dive and the longer you do it the bigger the risk of bone damage," says one veteran Aberdeen-based diver. "It's not an immediate fear among the lads, like the bends or hypothermia, or drowning, or even burning yourself with a welding torch. But it's always there at the back of your mind. Like smoking and cancer. After a few years at the game you start worrying about every little twinge in your shoulder, or cramp in your leg."

The report, compiled by the Decompression Fitness Central Registry at the university, and published by the Underwater Engineering Group, found that while none of the men who confined themselves to shallow water had bone damage, eight per cent who went below 100 metres had developed symptoms. Below 200 metres the figures shot up to 15.8 per cent, while more than 22 per cent of the men who had dived below 300 metres had bone lesions.

Professor Dennis Walder, one of the authors of the report, explained that bone necrosis attacks the arm and leg bones of the divers. So long as the lesions are confined to the "shaft" of the bone little damage is done but once X-rays show lesions in the diver's joints (usually the shoulder joints) the diver's fitness certificate is cancelled, and his well-paid underwater career is usually over.

No-one is quite sure why bone necrosis should plague men who work at great barometric pressures. "The traditional feeling is that the decompression process sets up bubbles from the body tissue," Walder explains, "and that somehow, these bubbles block the blood vessels supplying the bone so that the bone dies. But there are a number of problems with that theory. If it is that random, why does necrosis affect only the long bones like the femur and humerus? Why not the vertebrae or the fingers?"

And why bone necrosis should undermine the shoulder joints is equally puzzling. "All I can suggest," Walder says "is that because divers are supported by the water their legs do very little work. But their shoulders work hard. It could be that the action of the muscles draws blood away from the bones making it more vulnerable."

Nor can there be any "cure" for bone necrosis until the cause and effect of the condition is clearly understood. Since the early 1970s Walder and his colleagues have been working on the startling theory that the gas bubbles which do the damage are generated by spontaneous nuclear fission in the body, in a series of minuscule atomic explosions. "We think that this fission is fuelled by the small deposits of uranium 238 which we all carry in our bodies," he says. "It is significant, we think, that most of it is carried in the surface of our bones."

With the help of nuclear scientists from Harwell, Walder is trying to find some simple way of identifying people who carry large quantities of uranium so that they could be "screened out" from deep diving. "We haven't come up with anything yet," Walder says, "but we're working on it."

George Rosie

(From: *The Sunday Times*, 28 February 1982)

Sequential Notes

> **How divers' bones die 1,000 feet under (George Rosie,** *The Sunday Times,* **28 February 1982, p. 13).**
>
> ### Aseptic bone necrosis
> Report by Decompression Fitness Central Registry. University of Newcastle.
>
> 1. Symptoms
>   (a) attacks arms and legs
>   (b) little damage when in shaft of bone
>   (c) crippling when in joints
>
> 2. Incidence
>   on the increase as search for oil goes into deeper water:
>   8% below 100 m
>   15.8% below 200 m
>   22% below 300 m
>
> 3. Unanswered questions
>   (a) why affects long bones like femur and humerus?
>   (b) why affects shoulder joints?
>
> 4. Cure?
>   None until cause and effect understood.
>   Theory that it affects people with large quantities of uranium in their bodies.
>   No way of identifying these.

Nuclear Notes

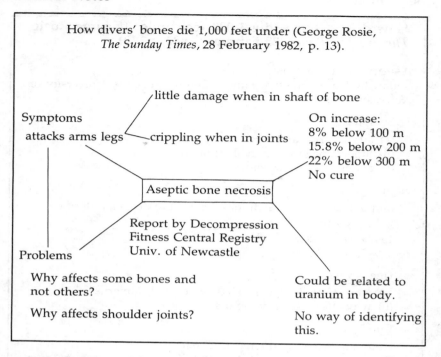

How divers' bones die 1,000 feet under (George Rosie, *The Sunday Times*, 28 February 1982, p. 13).

little damage when in shaft of bone

Symptoms
attacks arms legs — crippling when in joints

On increase:
8% below 100 m
15.8% below 200 m
22% below 300 m
No cure

Aseptic bone necrosis

Report by Decompression Fitness Central Registry Univ. of Newcastle

Problems

Why affects some bones and not others?

Why affects shoulder joints?

Could be related to uranium in body.

No way of identifying this.

Why dentists go on practising after deaths of patients

Two dentists who between them have been responsible for the deaths of three patients and for putting another in intensive care for three weeks are being allowed to continue to practise without restriction. Both acted against the repeated advice of the Department of Health and the British Dental Association in giving general anaesthetics alone. As yet, however, there has been no review of their professional behaviour.

Such cases are investigated by the General Dental Council – the professional watchdog – only if a formal complaint is made or when a conviction obtained in court stands beyond further appeal. By the time an appeal has been heard, a dentist may have continued in practice for years after a death in his surgery.

Kewal Abrol, 53, a dentist still practising as usual last week at Gravelly Hill, Birmingham, was found guilty of manslaughter at Stafford Crown Court last October. The court heard how a 52-year-old woman, Joyce Foundling, mother of two, died without regaining consciousness after he had given her a general anaesthetic to extract a tooth.

He gave the anaesthetic single-handed, without even a dental reception in the surgery, and at one point he left Mrs Foundling completely alone for 10 minutes. During this time, she choked on her own vomit.

Abrol was sentenced to 18 months' imprisonment, suspended for two years, and fined £1,000. After the verdict, it was disclosed in court that in 1973 another patient, Michael Seal, 18, had died in similar circumstances at Abrol's hands. Counsel for the defence said at the trial that Abrol would face a disciplinary hearing by the General Dental Council which would almost inevitably result in his name being struck off.

However, Abrol has appealed and it may be several months before all legal moves are exhausted. Even then, there could be a further delay of six months before the General Dental Council considers the case: it meets only twice a year.

Neil Forker, 29, a dentist at Egremont, Cumbria, gave an injection of contaminated anaesthetic to Paul Pickering, 25, a machine operator and father of two. The injection of methohexitone – a short-acting barbiturate drug – was subsequently found to have been mixed with halothane, an anaesthetic properly given only as a vapour.

Pickering had three teeth filled but became ill and was taken home by Forker. Later the same day, he fell very seriously ill and had to be taken to hospital.

Shortly afterwards Forker went ahead with an anaesthetic for a second patient, David McAllister, 20. Although he knew by then of Pickering's worsened condition, he used the same bottle of anaesthetic. McAllister, who was scheduled to have seven fillings, also became seriously ill and was taken to hospital.

Both men had to be put on life-support machines. Pickering died after 16 days.

An inquest on Pickering returned a verdict of accidental death. However, the inquest heard that the metal cap securing a rubber bung in the bottle of anaesthetic had been removed.

Normal professional safeguards were ignored in at least two respects: the dentist used a bottle that had been tampered with and so was no longer sterile; and the second dose was given from the bottle after one patient had suffered a serious and unexplained illness. Proper practice would be to use a drug from a fresh bottle if anything untoward had happened.

The police are now making further inquiries into Pickering's death. A formal complaint in connection with the case has been made to the General Dental Council but it has yet to decide whether there is a case to answer. If it does so decide, the hearing could take place in May, provided there are no legal reasons for postponing it.

It is 15 years since the Department of Health first advised dentists not to practise anaesthesia and operate at the same time. The two roles, it said, could not be combined without risk. This opinion was endorsed in 1975 by the British Dental Association and the president of the General Dental Council.

According to the latest figures, about 9 or 10 deaths a year are caused wholly or partly by dental anaesthesia, of which some occur in hospital.

Ronald Allen, secretary of the British Dental Association, says: "About a million dental anaesthetics are given each year. Most of the deaths are due to idiosyncracies in the patient which could not be determined beforehand. General anaesthetics should be given by a specialist anaesthetist but at present that is impracticable because there are not enough dentists with postgraduate training in anaesthesia. Any anaesthetic carries a risk."

Olivier Gillie

(From: *The Sunday Times*, 28 February 1982)

Now jot down your own notes on sheets of A4 paper, under the following headings:

Sequential Notes
Why dentists go on practising after deaths of patients (Oliver Gillie, *The Sunday Times*, 28 February 1982, p. 3).

Nuclear Notes
Why dentists go on practising after deaths of patients (Oliver Gillie, *The Sunday Times*, 28 February 1982, p. 3).

Keep your completed notes, which you may send to your tutor as part of Assignment E. .

3. CLASSIFICATION AND FILING

3.1 The purpose of filing
A pocket cartoon used to adorn the front of a filing cabinet in our office. A secretary, clutching a wodge of papers, was addressing her boss, 'Do you want this again, Sir, or shall I file it?'

Too many filing systems are like that. And the average person's ability to create a useful filing system is pretty low. The majority of people plump for the alphabetical system which, while simple, is not easy to use. Sets of notes can be classified under many headings and one has to search through at least two or three to find the necessary papers.

Retrieval, however, is what it's all about. We create filing systems in order to take information out at a later date.

Activity 24: Purposes of a filing system
Consider how information is set out in the following filing systems:

- *Telephone directory*
- *Atlas*
- *Library subject index*
- *Library author index.*

This activity emphasises that the design of a filing system depends entirely on what you are going to use it for.

A telephone directory is designed to tell us the number of a person whose name and initials we know (or in the case of the yellow pages, of a service we require). In this case the entries are alphabetical.

An atlas is designed to give us information about countries. The names of places are indexed in alphabetical order, so that we can quickly find out on which map they appear.

The two library indexes show how the *same* information can be organised in two *different* ways for different purposes. Books can be grouped under subjects or under author. We need the first index when we want to find out what books there are on a particular topic. We need the second index when we want to find out what a particular author wrote. And both indexes will tell us where a book has been placed by the library.

3.2 Natural and artificial classification
There are two basic classification systems, natural and artificial. Artficial classification groups material according to one characteristic only. For example, an artificial classification of people would be brought about by subdividing them into English speaking and non-English speaking. An artificial classification of animals might divide them into two-legged and other than two-legged. Artficial classifications are extremely sensitive to the single factor arbitrarily chosen for the classifying. As a result, artificial classification produces some odd results. The two-legged division of animals puts man and the sparrow in one division and cows and centipedes in another. Artificial schemes have their uses – nationality is an artificial classification.

A natural classification makes use of overall similarity. This leads us to divide people into men and women; dwellings into bungalows, houses, cottages, flats; living things into birds, mammals, plants etc. Although natural classifications are still somewhat arbitrary, they lead to a more uniform division of the material than do artificial schemes.

3.3 The alphabetical system (an artificial scheme)
The position of any item in an alphabetical system is determined purely by the accidents of language. In a library which classified its books alphabetically, books on Christmas and chrysanthemums would come close together, but books on roses would be many shelves away. As soon as the list of topics in such a system is more than can be read through in a minute or so, the alphabetical system becomes tedious.

As the amount of information you want to classify grows, it might be useful to use a semi-alphabetical system. Here you would have a heading (e.g. gardening) and underneath that heading topics (e.g. roses) would appear in alphabetical order.

Of course, the alphabetical system is ideal for material which does not need to be grouped, such as names in a telephone directory. But if you were a postman you would group the same people by street, not by name. Thus, in choosing a classification system you must bear in mind how and why you are going to retrieve information from it.

3.4 Subject classification (a natural scheme)

You will almost certainly want to classify the bulk of your notes by subject. For example, headings for a biologist might include:

> Physiology
> Ecology
> Vertebrates

But any classification system is arbitrary, and there will always be awkward cases. In the above system, where would you place notes on Vertebrate ecology? The answer is to place them under either Ecology or Vertebrates and then insert a cross-reference under the other heading. Thus:

> Physiology
> Ecology (*see* also Vertebrate ecology)
> Vertebrates
>   Vertebrate ecology

or

> Physiology
> Ecology
>   Vertebrate ecology
> Vertebrates (*see* also Ecology – Vertebrate ecology).

Activity 25: Creating a classification system
Design a filing system for:

- *your bills*
- *your personal correspondence.*

Start by writing down the purpose to which you are going to put the system. Only when that is absolutely clear in your mind will you be able to design a good system to meet your requirements.

3.5 Filing systems

Even when you have chosen a classification scheme for your notes, you will still need a way of putting that scheme into practice by finding a suitable filing system.

One of the best filing systems is the loose-leaf folder. It has many advantages over other systems:

- New material can be inserted at any point.
- Material can be subdivided with commercially made divisions (tabulated if necessary).
- The system can be endlessly expanded, if necessary beyond the original folder to a whole range of folders.
- Material can be reordered quickly.

To get the most out of a loose-leaf system you should only write on one side of the paper, and start new topics on new sheets of paper. Then any one topic can be removed, altered or reordered without upsetting other notes. Writing on one side only allows additions to be made opposite existing notes.

The loose-leaf system has so many advantages over the traditional notebook that it makes the notebook obsolete.

Where many different sorts of material are involved, the loose-leaf system may be inadequate. For example, if you have notes, pamphlets, maps, diagrams and press-cuttings, it may be difficult to place them all in ring-binders. In such circumstances, you may like to use large cardboard envelopes, or if you feel it is necessary, buy a filing cabinet and use filing folders.

3.6 Card Filing

Card filing is extremely useful for small items of information. Like the loose-leaf system, it is easily added to, amended and reordered. In addition, it is easy to index the cards by a clear entry in the top left-hand corner. The standard size of card is 13 × 8 cm but for handwritten work the larger sizes are also useful: 15 × 10 cm and 20 × 13 cm.

Card files are very useful when collating work for an essay. We will discuss the method in the next chapter, which deals with essay writing.

ASSIGNMENT D

This is your second MAIL test. Please pick options A to D (honestly!) for each of the following questions. Enter the letter of your choice for each question on a MAIL answer form, and return it direct to NEC.

1. When you make notes from text books, it is important to record the title, author, publisher, and place and date of publication; also the page numbers of particularly relevant sections. Which is the best reason for doing this as a matter of routine?

   A So that you can find the book again.

   B So that you can quote from the book without having to find it again.

   C So that you can keep track of which books you have already consulted.

   D So that you can list your reference sources in a bibliography if required.

2. When making notes from printed materials, it is often useful to re-draft important ideas in your own words. Why?

   A So that you won't be accused of 'cribbing' from the book if you include the ideas concerned in an essay or assignment.

   B Because it means that you think harder about the material concerned than you would have if you just copied it out.

   C So that you make an easy-to-read summary – easier to learn from than the original material.

   D To prevent you becoming a 'passive' reader.

3. Which is the best way to make notes at a lecture?

   A Try to write down everything the lecturer says, so that you can sort out what is important later.

   B Only write down the things most other people seem to be noting down; just sit there and listen when no-one else is writing.

   C Write down only the important ideas, missing out the finer detail.

   D Don't write anything during the lecture, but write out some notes later, 'in private'.

4. Suppose you are studying a topic, and deciding whether or not to buy a copy of a recommended textbook. Would you:

   A buy the book anyway?

   B look through the course material to see how often the book concerned was mentioned, before deciding?

   C borrow the book concerned from a library, and skim it to see how relevant it is, before deciding?

   D not consider the book unless the course materials themselves proved quite inadequate?

5. How much use do you think you will make of 'nuclear' notes?

 A Not much, because I prefer to write full sentences.

 B Not much, because the subjects I'm studying require sequential notes.

 C Quite a lot, I think, once I've got used to the technique.

 D I already use 'nuclear' notes.

6. How do you organise your notes? Which statement fits you best?

 A I prefer using notebooks rather than a loose-leaf system.

 B I use a loose-leaf file, but I use both sides of the paper; paper's expensive!

 C I use a loose-leaf file, and frequently rearrange the sheets into a more logical order (so I write on only one side).

 D I make notes on loose sheets of paper, but somehow I don't get round to filing the sheets systematically.

7. How has Unit 3 on 'Reading' affected you? Choose the statement which is nearest to your experience.

 A My reading has been revolutionised.

 B You've spoiled my reading! I keep trying to remember what I've read, even trivial stuff.

 C I'm being a lot more particular about what I choose to read now.

 D Old habits die hard. I'm reading more or less as I always did.

8. What effect has Unit 4 on Note-taking and Filing had on you?

 A Not a lot; I was always pretty good at these.

 B Tremendous! I now feel that I'm organised; before I was chaotic.

 C I can't really say yet – but I'm now full of good intentions.

 D I'm new to note-taking and filing; I think this unit reached me just at the right time.

The final two questions are to help us find out how useful (or otherwise) you are finding the MAIL assignments on this course.

9. Glance back at the feedback you received from the computer for Assignment B. How did you find the feedback comments?

 A Very helpful and relevant.

 B Quite useful.

 C Didn't seem to match my answers.

 D Not useful – a waste of time.

10. Did you notice anything about the speed of getting back your responses to Assignment B?

 A Yes, much quicker than tutor-marked assignments; this meant I got the feedback while the questions were still fresh in my mind.

 B Yes, much quicker than tutor-marked assignments, but it didn't make any real difference to me. ▶

C I didn't actually notice whether or not the assignment was handled more quickly.

D It doesn't matter to me how long it takes to get my work processed.

Never write about any matter that you do not well understand.

COBBETT

1. OBJECTIVES

When you have worked through this unit and carried out the activities you should be able to:

- understand the purpose of essays
- explain the importance of planning ahead
- decide exactly what is being asked for in an essay title
- collect information for essays and record that information in note form
- write an essay plan
- explain what makes a readable style of writing for an essay
- write clear paragraphs
- use quotations effectively
- present an essay for evaluation.

2. THE PURPOSE OF ESSAYS

- Essays are simply a convenient way of expressing your ideas. If you can *talk* clearly and logically, and interest your listeners, you should be able to do the same in writing. Writing is just a more permanent form of communication. Provided you really believe this you should have no difficulty in writing effective essays.
- Essays help you to understand and learn a topic. They encourage you to revise the notes you have taken.
- Essays give you and your tutors the opportunity to see if you have understood the material presented in class.
- Exams entail writing essays, and you need practice in this.
- Essays make sure you work *throughout* a course and not just before an exam.
- In 'continuous assessment', the marks your tutor awards for your essays contribute to your final grading.

3. ESSAY WRITING

An essay can be very time-consuming. You should *plan ahead* and set yourself deadlines for each of the major stages. A detailed analysis of each of these stages is given in the rest of this section.

Suppose an essay topic is given to you on 15 March and is due at the end of April – a period of six weeks. A typical plan might be:

Week 1: Choose the topic (*see* Section 3.1), analyse it (3.2), record known information and ask questions (3.3.1). Ask the tutor to explain any instructions that you do not understand. Find out the meaning of any specialist terms in the question.

Week 2: Decide on sources (3.3.2). This will involve a search through your own books, and trips to the libraries available to you. You will have to skim through your sources quickly to see if you have sufficient information. If not, you may have to plan a trip to another library or send for books.

Week 3: Record the information (3.3.3)
Week 4: Make an outline plan (3.4) and write up the penultimate draft
Week 5: (3.5).
Week 6: Write out the essay for presentation (3.6).

3.1 Stage one: choice of topic

In exams and tests you will normally find yourself with a choice of topic to write on. Choose a topic which you know and understand well, rather than something new and unfamiliar. If you have no choice and find yourself committed to an unfamiliar topic, read about that topic before you even begin to plan your essay or make notes for it. If you can't understand a topic before you write on it, you will be unable to select material for inclusion or develop a logical argument around the material you select.

3.2 Stage two: analysing the topic

Your starting point is your title or topic. Many students have put hours of effort into their own interpretation of an allotted topic. Titles are your marching orders. Follow them and you are well on the way to a good essay. Here are some examples of related essay topics each of which demands very different treatment from the others:

1. Describe the constitutional crisis which led to the Civil War.
2. Cromwell: democrat or dictator?
3. How could Charles I have saved his throne and head?

The first topic is largely descriptive, although it demands some interpretation of events. You would, for example, have to select those events which you consider brought about the crisis and reject other incidental occurrences.

Superficially, the other two titles relate to the same events. But one concentrates on Cromwell and the other on Charles I. Note also that the most controversial part of Cromwell's life follows the death of Charles I. Thus the second two topics cover different periods of history. Another point to note is that whereas the first topic is largely descriptive, the second asks you to interpret events, and the third asks you to imagine alternative events. For many students the danger is to see all three titles as one topic: the Civil War. As a result they pour out their textbook knowledge of the events of the Civil War and neglect the special emphasis of the essay title.

To help yourself analyse the topic, it is a good idea to underline the *key words*. These can be described as the important words, and give the essential information. They can:

- tell you how to proceed (e.g. the word 'describe' in Topic 1 above). (There is an appendix at the end of this unit which will help you work out what certain standard key words mean. You may find it useful as a source of reference in your future studies.)
- help you to collect material which is relevant (e.g. the terms 'constitutional crisis' and 'civil war' in Topic 1 above. You would have to collect information on both of these.)

The following activity illustrates this point.

Activity 26: What the title asks for

Here are three essay titles:

1. *Discuss whether the Japanese should be allowed to kill dolphins in Japanese waters.*
2. *Justify the compulsory teaching of domestic science to boys as well as girls.*
3. *Explain why lead should be banned from petrol.*

First *underline the key words,*
then *decide which of the following items are relevant to the titles:*

- *What we mean by 'compulsory'.*
- *The meaning of 'discuss'.*
- *The effects of lead in the air on health.*
- *The meaning of 'justify'.*
- *The effects of dolphins on the Japanese fishing industry.*
- *The future tasks in society of boys and girls.*
- *The effect of banning lead on the price of petrol.*
- *The rights of some countries to interfere in the internal matters of other countries.*
- *The damage done by the Japanese in World War II.*
- *The sorts of food preparation that should be included on a school syllabus.*
- *Examples of countries which have banned lead in petrol.*
- *The meaning of 'explain'.*

There are no absolutely right answers to this activity. An ingenious writer can relate apparently unconnected items. However, students do not have such 'poetic licence'. The golden rule of essay writing is *only introduce information which you can relate to the title*, and this may involve leaving out lots of information that you know.

The words I underlined are:

1. Discuss whether the Japanese should be allowed to kill dolphins in Japanese waters.
2. Justify the compulsory teaching of domestic science for boys as well as girls.
3. Explain why lead should be banned from petrol.

3.3 Stage three: collecting information

3.3.1 Task 1: Record known information and ask questions
Your first task is to write down what you already know on the subject. Then you should ask questions to which you hope to find answers in your books. (Here you may like to use sequential and/or nuclear notes – *see* Unit 4, Section 2.5.)

Activity 27: Recording known information and asking questions
1. *Look again at Question 1 in Activity 26:*

   '*Discuss whether the Japanese should be allowed to kill dolphins in Japanese waters.*'

   Known information might include:

   - *Dolphins are a protected species in most parts of the world.*
   - *There is a strong lobby group in America and Britain whose aim is to protect dolphins.*
   - *The Japanese fishermen are poor and kill the dolphins because they eat their fish.*

   Questions to answer might include:

   - *Are dolphins an endangered species or are their numbers on the increase?*
   - *How far do Japanese waters extend?*
   - *Are there international rules about killing dolphins?*
   - *Are there unusually high concentrations of dolphins in Japanese waters?*

2. *Using the above example as a guide, list:*
   - *known information for Questions 2 and 3.*
   - *questions to be answered for Questions 2 and 3 in Activity 26.*

3.3.2 Task 2: Decide on sources
You now have to decide where you are going to look to collect the information.

(a) Look at any notes you have on this subject. This will help you recall known information.

(b) Has your tutor given you any titles of books and/or articles on the topic?

(c) Are there any titles on your general reading list which could be useful?

(d) Use the library index:
   - Look in the *subject catalogue* for the topic. If there are many books on this topic, then find the most appropriate subtitle.
   - If you know that a particular author specialises in this topic, look in the *author catalogue*.

- Look up the *periodicals indexes* to find a recent article on this topic. When/if you find an article which is particularly relevant, look at the bibliography if there is one. This will lead you to other references.

  (If your topic has been chosen by lots of students, and the books and periodicals you need are already borrowed, you will have to ask the library to recall them for you as soon as possible.)

(e) Use all available sources of information. Don't forget that there are sources other than books and periodicals (e.g. radio and television programmes). Discussions with others doing the same course may be useful, too.

3.3.3 Task 3: Record the information

It is important at this stage that you read quickly (*see* Unit 3 Section 3.1) and take appropriate notes (*see* Unit 4 Section 2.3). There are many ways of recording information. Two of them are suggested below.

Suggestion A: index cards

(i) On one side of each card record:
  - author
    title of the article (if in a journal or newspaper)
    title of the publication (if a book, journal, newspaper)
    the edition, if not the first edition
    publisher
    place of publication
    date of publication
    chapter and page number.

(ii) On the other side of the card put down *one* important point or quotation. You can then shuffle these cards into the order needed for your essay, and add to them easily.

Index Card

Side One

Buzan Tony ———————	Author
Use Your Head ———————	Title
BBC Publications ———————	Publisher
London ———————	Place of publication
1974 ———————	Date of publication
Ch. 4 ———————	Chapter
p. 41 ———————	Page number

The books and periodicals you need are already borrowed . . .

> 'The entire Organic Study Method must be seen not as a step-by-step progression but as a series of inter-related aspects of approaching study material.'

Suggestion B: sheets of paper

    (i) Use one (or more) sheets for your bibliography. Number each of your sources and record the details given above for side one of the index card.

    (ii) On the top of each of the other sheets write down one specific question for which you require information.

As we have already suggested in Unit 4 Section 2.3, use a code number to indicate the source of each piece of information. Thus 2,32 would mean that the point occurred on page 32 of the book numbered 2 on your bibliography sheet.

By using this system of separate sheets for notes on separate topics you will find that by the time you have finished your reading you will have a preliminary sorting of your material. This 'purposeful' reading will also result in fewer, more relevant notes.

The following example illustrates this method:

Sheets of Paper

Sheet 1

Bibliography

1. Buzan, Tony, *Use your head.* BBC Publications, London, 1974.
2. Gibbs, Graham. *Teaching students to learn.* Open University Press, Milton Keynes, 1981.
3. Hills, P. J. and Barlow, H. *Effective study skills.* Pan, London, 1980.
4. Main, Alex. *Encouraging effective learning.* Scottish Academic Press, Edinburgh, 1980.

> **Question** What are the different ways of making notes?
>
> Write down the key points (3, 50).
>
> 'Taking notes from a book makes different demands from taking notes from packaged learning materials' (2, 18).
>
> You must decide your purpose before taking notes (4, 44).
>
> Organic notes (1, 88).

> **Question** How can you read more effectively and faster?
>
> Quantity of material can overwhelm students (2, 24).
>
> Read words in meaningful groups (3, 29).
>
> 'The most significant question I have ever asked any student who confesses difficulty with reading comprehension is, "Would you like to tell me about the different kinds of reading your course demands?"' (4, 39).
>
> Definition of reading: 'Reading is the individual's total inter-relationship with symbolic information' (1, 24).

3.4 Stage four: Making an outline plan

An outline is a series of headings with an idea or two under each heading. But basically it consists of headings. The outline headings should do no more than cover the points you intend to write about.

The priority in the outline is logical order. This does not mean that there is one and only one order which you can consider, but it does mean that your final order must justify itself and be seen to do so by the reader.

One way of doing this is to look at the material you have collected and decide which point is most important. You might make this your conclusion. Then sort out three or more other main points which you will expand. Your plan would then look like this:

- *Introduction:* define your terms and indicate how you intend to tackle the topic.

  Main body: the main points – ideas and arguments together with illustrations or examples.

  Conclusion: your final point – recall the issues raised in the introduction, draw together the points you made in the main body, and explain the overall significance of your conclusions.

Length: A limitation on your outline is length. If you are set a limit of 2,000 words you will have to be far more selective than for 5,000 words. Make sure that you take this into account at the outline stage. If you don't, you will have to replan when the essay is half written.

If you are given a limit of 2,000 words, you might split it up thus:

- Introduction   250 words or less
  Main body   1,200–1,400 words. Allow equal wording for each main point.
  Conclusion   500 words or so.

Activity 28: Essay outlines

Here is an outline for an essay 'Should sex education be taught in schools'?

Introduction
- *(a) What is sex education?*
- *(b) How important is it?*
- *(c) Who should teach it, parents or teachers?*

Main body
- *(a) Arguments for sex education in schools.*
  - *Part 1. Many children do not receive sex education in their homes. (Back up with evidence.)*
  - *Part 2. Children get misinformation from each other. (Give an example.)*
  - *Part 3. Sex education involves many aspects of health and hygiene. (Give an example.)*
  - *Part 4. Children able to ask questions about aspects they do not understand. (Give an example.)*
  - *Part 5. No evidence that sex education promotes promiscuity. (Back up with evidence.)*

- *(b) Arguments against sex education in schools.*
  - *Part 1. Parents have right to decide what sex education their children receive. (Can agree or disagree with this. Compare with other subjects.)*
  - *Part 2. Teachers not trained for the task. (Back up with evidence.)*
  - *Part 3. Children become embarrassed during sex education lessons. (Back up with evidence.)*

Conclusion
This will depend on the evidence presented in the main body. Make a definite statement. Recall and draw together the main arguments.

Now make your own outline for one of the following topics:
- *Should protective clothing be worn by school cricketers?*
- *Should the government support private schools financially?*

3.5 Stage five: Writing the penultimate draft

It is a good idea to draft your essay first, in order to get down all the necessary information. This enables you to strengthen arguments and improve your structure and writing style before writing the final version.

3.5.1 Style

Everyone worries about style when writing. Good style involves saying what you want to say clearly and concisely. Pompous language, excessively long or complex sentences, hackneyed phrases, clichés, are to be rejected.

To be ruthless is difficult. We are surrounded by pompous English which is frequently encouraged by officials as *good* English.

Consider the policeman:

'I was proceeding down the High Street when I apprehended the said defendant in the act of purloining a motor vehicle on the Queen's Highway.'

All he means is that he saw Mr. Jones stealing a car in the High Street.

Or the businessman:

'The non-compensable evaluation heretofore assigned to you for your service-connected disability is confirmed and continued.'

(What he means is anyone's guess.)

Improving your style is not so much a question of textbooks or exercises as it is of wide reading. And beware of the tendency to wrap up a poor argument in verbose phrases and rambling paragraphs.

Of course there are occasions when 'jargon' is necessary to convey a precise meaning. The social sciences require 'jargon' to avoid the looser type of thinking which we use in everyday life. But on the whole, simplicity is the key to clarity.

3.5.2 Paragraphs

Remember:

- Each paragraph usually deals with *one* idea or statement.
- The logic of your outline is carried through by the logic of you paragraphs.
- If you are uncertain which idea or statement one particular paragraph deals with, scrap or modify that paragraph. If *you* can't understand the logic of your argument, your readers won't stand a chance.

Activity 29: Paragraphing

Here is part of an article from The Observer *(8 March 1982). There were originally four paragraphs, but it has been reprinted all as one. Where did the original paragraphs begin and end?*

A Student in Moscow

Andrea Lee, a black American Harvard graduate, spent a year at Moscow State University in 1978. She and her husband, Tom, lived the life of ordinary Muscovites, queueing for food, travelling by metro. This is an extract from the unique journal she kept.

The Tower in which Tom and I will live for most of the next 10 months is one of the landmarks of Moscow, an absurd 32-storey wedding cake of grey and red granite, set above the city in the Lenin Hills. This titanic building, the main dormitory of Moscow State University, is a monument of the pompous and energetic style of architecture nicknamed 'Stalin Gothic'. Seen from a distance, it suggests a Disney version of a ziggurat; its central spire, like the Kremlin towers, holds a blinking red star. Standing beyond the customs barrier at Sheremetyevo Airport had been a young man who introduced himself in English as Grigorii, a journalism student sent to escort us by the university's office of foreign affairs. Grigorii was a dark-haired young man in his twenties, with very small eyes behind enormous round glasses and a pinched, rather gnomish body in a large, baggy suit; the impression he gave was that he had melted down slightly inside his clothing. When Grigorii left us, we flicked a switch, and in the sudden bright light, faced our living quarters for the year. They were what Russians call a *blok* – a minute suite consisting of two rooms about six feet by ten feet each, a tiny entryway, and a pair of cubicles containing, between them, a toilet, a shower and washstand, and several large, indolent cockroaches. The two main rooms were painted the dispiriting beige and green of institutional rooms around the world, and furnished, rather nicely, with varnished chairs, tables, bookcases, and two single beds. (I've since discovered that our rooms represent great luxury, since Russian students in the same building often live four and six to such quarters.) Each room held a radio that tuned in to only one station – Radio Moscow – and at this particular moment, news was being broadcast by a woman with an excited, throaty voice. The news went off, and on came a medley of Komsomol songs delivered stalwartly by what sounded like an entire nation of ruddy-cheeked young patriots. 'You can't turn this thing off.' said Tom, fiddling with the radio knob. Indeed, like one of Orwell's telescreens, our official radios could be turned down to inaudible, but never turned off.

Answers:

Paragraph 1 'The tower ………. red star'.

Paragraph 2 'Standing ………. inside his clothing'.

Paragraph 3 'When Grigorii left us ………. to such quarters'.

Paragraph 4 'Each room held .... but never turned off'.

If your answer was different to this you weren't necessarily 'wrong': there is usually more than one possible way to divide up a piece of writing.

3.5.3 Diagrams and illustrations

Some tutors discourage diagrams and illustrations in essays. Others, sensibly, welcome diagrams because they are easier to mark and are a fairer way of testing knowledge in subjects where writing skills are less important. However, there is no virtue in using or not using diagrams. The simple rule is to use whichever approach best explains your ideas. If a diagram is needed, insert it. If it is not needed, leave it out. For example, you might need to use illustrations in some of the following circumstances:

Essay subject	Possible illustrations/diagrams
Chemistry	Formulae
	Diagrams of models
	Charts, tables
	Pictures of apparatus
Geography	Maps
	Charts
	Graphs
Mathematics	Charts
	Formulae
	Graphs
History/Social Sciences	Maps
	Charts
	Tables
	Graphs

3.5.4 Quotations

If you use quotations it is important to weave them into your own argument. Remember, they must serve your own purposes and should be interpreted by you. This is easier with short quotations; the longer the quotation the harder it is to integrate it.

You may find it useful to use longer quotations in these two ways:

● To introduce some new view. This can create interest and emphasise a major point.

- To sum up an argument. Be sure that it relates to the earlier points you have made.

However, always bear in mind that quotations should never be used as a short cut to save writing down an explanation or argument of your own. In the end, it's always *your* ideas that count!

3.6 Stage six: Writing the finished essay

Your finished essay should be clear, tidy and legible.

The following points will help you:

- Use a typewriter if possible, with double spacing between lines for easier marking.
- If you are writing by hand, ask a friend to read your work to make sure it is legible, and to check for errors in spelling and grammar.
- Use one side of the paper only. (This prevents type showing through from the other side.)
- Leave a generous margin (about 4cm) on the left-hand side (and bottom) of the page, for your tutor's comments.
- Number the pages consecutively and pin them together.
- Include a title page. This should specify:
    The title of the essay
    The writer's name
    The course for which the essay is submitted
    The date of presentation.
- Include a bibliography. This should list all (if any) of the sources consulted.
- Always keep a copy of your essay in case the original gets lost.

Essay writing summary

Rather than summarise what I have said, I leave the task to eight Italian boys with little education but lots of sense:

'To start with each of us keeps a notebook in his pocket. Every time an idea comes up, we make a note of it. Each idea on a separate sheet, on one side of the page.

Then one day we gather all the sheets of paper and spread them on a big table. We look through them, one by one, to get rid of duplications. Next, we make separate piles of the sheets that are related, and these will make up the chapters. Every chapter is subdivided into small piles, and they will become paragraphs.

At this point we try to give a title to each paragraph. If we can't it means either that the paragraph has no content or that too many things are squeezed into it. Some paragraphs disappear. Some are broken up. While we name the paragraphs we discuss their logical order, until an outline is born. With the outline set, we reorganise all the piles to follow its pattern.

We take the first pile, spread the sheets on the table, and we find the sequence for them. And so we begin to put down a first draft of the text. We duplicate that part so that we each can have a copy in front of us. Then, scissors, paste and coloured pencils. We shuffle it all again. New sheets are added. We duplicate again.

A race begins now for all of us to find any word that can be crossed out, any excess adjectives, repetitions, lies, difficult words, over-long sentences, and any two concepts that are forced into one sentence.

We call in one outsider after another. We prefer it if they have not had too much schooling. We ask them to read aloud. And we watch to see if they have understood what we meant to say.

We accept their suggestions if they clarify the text. We reject any suggestions made in the name of caution.

Having done all this hard work and having followed these rules that anyone can use, we often come across an intellectual idiot who announces, "This letter has a remarkably personal style."

Why don't you admit that you don't know what the art of writing is? It is an art that is the very opposite of laziness.'

Quoted on the inside front cover of *Letter to a teacher* by the School of Barbiana. English translation in Penguin Books, 1970.

ASSIGNMENT E

This is the last of your tutor-marked assignments, and is a very important one. It has two sections, one on Unit 4 (Note-taking and Filing) and the other on the unit you have just completed, Unit 5 on Essay Writing. Please choose ONE question from EACH section, and send your work to your tutor. Please note that Section A contains shorter questions.

Section A: choose one question. Your answer should be 1–2 pages long.

1. Send your tutor your nuclear and sequential notes on the article 'Why dentists go on practising after the deaths of patients'.

OR

2. Discuss the way you made notes from a particular textbook, describing the sort of notes you used, how you used them, and why you used the method(s) you did.

OR

3. Describe the sort of filing system you use, and discuss any changes you intend to make after studying Unit 4.

Section B: choose one question. Your answer this time should be more substantial, maybe 4–5 pages or so.

4. Choose one of the statements below as the basis for an essay:
    (a) 'Political demonstrations should not be held in city streets'
    (b) 'All tobacco advertising should be banned'
    (c) 'Britain should not have any nuclear weapons'
    (d) 'Caning should be used in schools'
    (e) 'Mothers should always get custody of children after a divorce'.
Using the guidelines in Section 3 of Unit 5, do each of the following with your selected topic, and send your tutor the things you write in each:
   • analyse the topic by underlining the key words
   • record known information, and ask questions about the topic
   • list your sources, and record information using index cards or sheets of paper
   • write down a plan, including lists of arguments for and against the statement
   • decide on your 'side' or conclusion
   • write up the topic as an essay.
(Please don't forget to send your tutor your work on all of these parts, not just the final essay. Your tutor wishes to see the way you built up the essay).

5. Find at least three different articles in newspapers about one particular topic. Choose a topic that really interests you, and on which you have views of your own. Do each of the following things, sending your tutor each, plus of course the articles you based your work on.
   - devise an essay question on the topic
   - analyse your question by underlining key words
   - record known information, and ask questions about the topic
   - record information from the articles using index cards or sheets of paper
   - make a plan for the essay
   - write the essay.

APPENDIX 1: SOME KEY WORDS DEFINED

This appendix is based on one contained in *How to write essays* by Roger Lewis, published by the National Extension College, Cambridge.

Some of the terms that are frequently used in essay questions are listed below. Make sure that you are quite clear about the precise meaning of each of them. Use this list to refer back to later in your studies.

Compare	Look for similarities and differences between; *perhaps* reach a conclusion about which is preferable.
Contrast	Set in opposition in order to bring out differences.
Criticise	Give your judgement about (the merit of theories or opinions or the truth of facts); back your judgement by reasoning or a discussion of evidence.
Define	Set down the precise meaning of (a word or phrase). *In some cases it may be necessary or desirable to examine different possible, or often used, definitions.*
Discuss	Investigate or examine by argument; sift and debate; give reasons for and against; *also* examine the implications of.
Describe	Give a detailed or graphic account of.
Distinguish **Differentiate**	Look for the differences between.
Evaluate	Make an appraisal of the worth of (something) in the light of its truth or usefulness.
Explain	Make plain; interpret and account for; give reasons for.
Illustrate	Make clear and explicit.
Interpret	(Often means much the same as **illustrate**.)
Justify	Show adequate grounds for decisions or conclusions; answer the main objections likely to be made to them.
Outline	Give the main features or general principles of (a subject), omitting minor details and emphasising structure and arrangement.
Relate	(a) Narrate – more usual in exams. (b) Show how things are connected to each other, and to what extent they are alike, or affect each other.
State	Present in a brief, clear form.
Summarise	Give a concise account of the chief points of (a matter), omitting details and examples.
Trace	Follow the development or history of (a topic) from some point of origin.

UNIT 6

REVISION AND EXAMS

The best way to become familiar with a subject is to study it for an exam.

ANON

1. OBJECTIVES

When you have worked through this unit and carried out the related activities you should be able to:

- plan regular revision sessions in your timetable
- revise and shorten your notes
- check the regulations and syllabus for the course
- make a revision plan for your course(s)
- write exam answers in outline form
- write model answers
- list the best strategies for taking an exam.

There are two stages in preparing for an exam.

- Revising the material.
  Here the emphasis is on *content*. You need to be familiar with all the material set for the exam.
- Preparing for the exam itself.
  Here the emphasis is on *technique*. You need to know the type of examination for which you are preparing and what you will be expected to do in the exam room.

2. REVISION

The following ideas will help you revise your work.

2.1 Revise constantly

Many students regard revision as something they do in the last week or two before their exams. Revision of that kind is simply cramming and is not to be encouraged. It violates the principles of understanding which are dealt with in Unit 2. Instead of this last-minute cramming (i.e. attempting to learn material which has never been properly understood), your revision should be a regular process throughout the course.

There are three reasons for this:

- There is not enough time at the end of a course to revise all the material adequately.
- If you revise regularly you can ensure that your notes are complete.
- Constant revision will make new material easier to learn, as you will have understood the previous material on which it was based.

2.2 Start final revision early

About six weeks before the exam, make new, shortened notes from your original notes. This has two benefits:

- It will provide you with a set of condensed notes for your final revision.
- The act of shortening the notes is an active form of learning. This form of learning is not only more effective (*see* Unit 2) but is also more interesting.

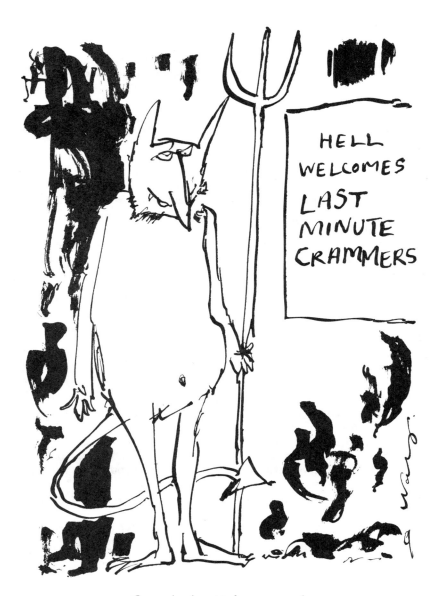

HELL
WELCOMES
LAST
MINUTE
CRAMMERS

Cramming is not to be encouraged.

2.3 Check the rules

You should have done this at the beginning of your course, but *recheck* them now

- to see if you have submitted all the required assignments
- to check exam regulations, e.g. Do you have to register separately for the exams? When are they? What times? How long?

2.4 Check the syllabus

Make sure you have notes on all the topics in the syllabus. If you think you have missed something check with your tutor.

2.5 Set up a revision group

One very good way to revise is to meet regularly (about twice a week) with two or three fellow students. This has the following benefits:

- It is a form of motivation. If you have set topics for each session, then you will be pressured to prepare them beforehand.
- It will help to make sure that you have not overlooked any important areas in the syllabus.
- You can teach each other.

Teaching someone else is a sure way of making you understand the material.

2.5 Make out a revision timetable

Use the chart on page 91 and

- write down the date
  - time
  - length of each exam
- put in the lectures which lead up to the exam (the lecturers often give hints on the exam at these!)
- put in your revision topics (allow for repeating a topic)
- keep one day a week free for a complete break. This is something you'll be able to look forward to and will provide your brain with some well-earned, and essential, relaxation
- keep a separate column for each subject. Tick off the topic when you have revised it
- use weeks 1–4 for general revision and week 5 for final revision.

Activity 30: Revision for exams

(This activity should not be done until six weeks before an actual exam.)

1. *Reread Section 2.*
2. *Follow the suggestions made.*

Revision Timetable					
Week ending		Day	e.g. Sociology	e.g. Mathematics	e.g. History
16 June		Mon Tues Wed Thurs Fri Sat Sun		 FREE	
23 June	GENERAL REVISION	Mon Tues Wed Thurs Fri Sat Sun		 FREE	
30 June	GENERAL REVISION	Mon Tues Wed Thurs Fri Sat Sun		 FREE	
7 July		Mon Tues Wed Thurs Fri Sat Sun		 FREE	
14 July	FINAL REVISION	Mon Tues Wed Thurs Fri Sat Sun		 FREE	
21 July	FINAL REVISION	Mon Tues Wed Thurs Fri Sat Sun	 Exam 9.00–12.00	Exam 1.30–4.30	 Exam 9.00–12.00

3. PREPARATION FOR EXAMS

Now that you have planned your revision you will have to plan for the exam itself by:

3.1 Examining the exam

Long before you take your exam it is essential to know just what sort of exam it is. You will need to check with your tutor or lecturer on a number of points:

- How many questions are there?
- What type of questions? – essay questions, problems, factual listings, multiple choice, practical exams, oral exams.
- How much choice will you have? This is very important if you can't finish the course before you start your revision. With sufficient choice you can safely omit one or two topics from your course.

Activity 31: Following the exam instructions

Match the correct explanations to the following instructions:

(i) Answer in note form

(a) All the marks are equally divided between the questions. To get full marks you must do all the questions.

(ii) Answer all questions

(b) You only get a mark for a tick in the right place. There are no marks for notes at the side. These notes will be ignored and waste valuable time.

(iii) Answer only five questions

(c) There are no marks for good English or well-phrased arguments. There are not many marks for this question. Don't spend too long on it.

(iv) Tick the correct answer from the following options

(d) You have to answer four questions to get full marks but one of them must be Question 1.

(v) Either ...... or ......

(e) You can't assume all the questions carry equal marks, so you must cover them all.

(vi) Answer Question 1 and three others

(f) Full marks can be scored, for either part. If you answer both, only the first one will be marked.

Answers at the end of the chapter.

3.2 Practising for exams

This can be done in three stages:

- Get hold of old exam papers *or* using the syllabus write up some mock questions for yourself (or ask your group). Collect questions together according to topics and use them when revising.
- Practise writing answers in outline form (*see* Unit 5 Section 3.4).

and/or

Discuss your outline with your revision group. It is a good idea for each member to answer the same question so that different approaches can be discussed. The group could also make up different questions for each other on a single topic.

- Write model answers.

Don't just look at the questions and say to yourself, 'Yes I could do this one, no I can't do that one', but actually *practise* writing model answers.

However efficiently and effectively you have studied your course, exams will be different. The major difference is working to time. So, practise at least two papers under strict examination conditions. Allow yourself only the normal exam time and only those materials which you are allowed to take into the exam. This will also show you how much you can actually get done in the time and help you to plan your allocation of time within the exam itself. It will also reveal to you the extent to which you've mastered your course and it may show you that further revision and practice work are needed. For this reason make sure that your first practice exam is at least one month before the real exam.

Activity 32: Practising for exams

(This activity should not be done until two weeks before an actual exam.)

1. *Reread Section 3.2.*
2. *Work through the three stages outlined there.*

3.3 The exam itself

3.3.1 The day before
Check, and tick off when you've done so:
- ☐ The place of the exam. (Be *sure* you know how to get there.)
- ☐ The starting time.
- ☐ Your candidate number.
- ☐ Your equipment:
    - ☐ Pens
    - ☐ Pencil
    - ☐ Rubber
    - ☐ Watch
    - ☐ Paper (if needed)
    - ☐ Slide rule
    - ☐ Calculator

Add your own ideas. ☐   ☐   ☐

3.3.2 In the examination room
If you have a chance, choose an area where there is plenty of light and where you can see the clock clearly. Check your watch with the clock.

3.3.3 Tackling the paper
(a) Check that it is the correct one (There may be other exams taking place in the room.)

(b) Fill in your personal details
Put your name, candidate number and any other details required on your exam booklet.

(c) Read the instructions carefully
- How many questions are you asked to do?
- Are any compulsory?
- Do different sections have to be done in separate booklets?
- Are there objective test questions?
- Where must the answers be written?

(d) Choose your questions
- Put a light pencil mark through those questions you can't possibly attempt.
- Put a tick at the side of those you can definitely do.
- Number the ticked questions from easiest to hardest. Do the easy ones first; this will give you confidence and allow more time for the more difficult questions later.

(e) Check your questions
Reread the questions you have ticked, and note the key words (*see* Unit 5 Section 3.2 and Appendix 1 p. 86).

(f) Make notes for each question
Points will flood into your memory in a random way. Switch from

one question to another, jotting down the ideas that come to mind. Use the mnemonics you practised in Unit 2 Section 4.4.

(g) Ration your time
- If the questions have equal marks give them equal time.
- Jot down a mini-timetable for your chosen questions, e.g.:
- Quick notes on chosen questions 9.00– 9.30
  - Q.1 9.30–10.10
  - Q.4 10.10–10.50
  - Q.6 10.50–11.30 etc.

If you run short of time, do remember that you can't get more than full marks on a question (and rarely as much as that). So a good pass requires answers to as many questions as the examiners tell you to answer. For example, suppose there are 100 marks and you have to do five questions. If you do three well (say 14 out of 20 for each) you get 42 marks – not enough to pass if the pass mark is 50. But if you can get 4 out of 20 on each of two other questions, you would pass. This illustrates an important point: if you haven't done your full quota of questions and are short of time, use that time to write short notes on the remainder of your quota. In this way you should be able to show the examiner more of your knowledge than by a more elaborate answer to one question.

(h) Tackle each question in turn. Write clear, precise answers.
Be careful not to over-answer. Each question should take no longer than the time allowed by the examiners, but too often candidates take longer because they exceed the question. So, if a question is taking more than its fair share of time, reread the question – you may not be answering it.

(i) When you have finished the paper:
- Read through all your answers. Check for omissions, poor spelling and illegible phrases. Search your mind for any last-minute points. (Better to do it then, than to remember them after the exam is over.)
- Check that your name is on *each* page.
- Number each page and clip any loose sheets together.

3.3.4 After the exam
Do not waste time in 'post-mortems'. You have done all you can. Go out and relax.

Answers to Activity 31: (i)–(c), (ii)–(e), (iii)–(a), (iv)–(b), (v)–(f), (vi)–(d).

ASSIGNMENT F

This is the last assignment on the course. It deals with revision strategies and exam technique. Please make your choices from the options given, entering the letter of your choice on the form as usual. Don't forget to send this form direct to NEC.

1. Revision often has to be fitted in alongside other course work – and indeed alongside the rest of the things that make up your life. Which of the patterns below will make sure you get plenty of revision done?
   A Do half an hour of revision first, then do all the other urgent tasks.
   B Get the urgent tasks out of the way, so that you can then concentrate on revision.
   C Make a rigid revision schedule, doing some every day.
   D Leave a solid two weeks before the exam for revision and no other work.

2. How well you know something depends a lot on how you have revised it. Which strategy below do you think gives the best results?
   A Reading through everything in the last few weeks before the exam.
   B Making revision summaries in the last few weeks.
   C Using your revision summaries often during the last few weeks.
   D Planning a timetable so you go through each revision summary once in the last few weeks.

3. Dave is an intelligent student. He has attended every lecture, and knows the main ideas in his lecture notes thoroughly. Dave hasn't done much reading around the material of his course, he's just stuck to 'getting to grips' with his lecture notes. What do you think Dave's score is likely to be, on average, in his exams?
   A 55%
   B 70%
   C 85%
   D 95%

4. Suppose you're revising, and you come across one concept that you simply can't understand. The exam is looming up, and you suspect that there will be one question on that concept. What would you do?
   A Struggle with the concept, until you finally get it to make sense to you.
   B Spend a few minutes each day trying to get to grips with the concept, but revising all the rest of the material as well.
   C Ignore the concept, and concentrate on consolidating the things you can understand.
   D Panic, and give up altogether, because that concept has defeated you.

5. Suppose a syllabus contains 8 topics, all about the same length and standard. Suppose the exam paper will contain one question on each topic, and that 5 questions (*any* 5) are to be attempted in the exam. Suppose for the sake of argument that Alison learns all 8 topics at about 60% efficiency, and that Brenda learns only five topics, but at about 80% efficiency. What do you think will happen in the exam?

    A Alison gets about 60%, Brenda gets about 80%

    B Alison gets about 60%, Brenda gets between 60% and 70%.

    C Alison gets about 60%, Brenda gets rather less than 60%.

    D It's more complicated than any of these!

6. It's very important to read each exam question slowly, calmly, and several times, before starting to write. When candidates don't do this, disasters happen. Which do you think are the commonest disasters, which would have been avoided if the candidates had read the questions as I suggest above?

    A Question misinterpreted, good answer content, but few marks as it doesn't answer the question.

    B Candidate could do the first bit of the question, but didn't realise till too late that he couldn't answer the most important part.

    C Candidate dived straight into the question, spent 10 minutes on it, then realised that a different question was better for her, so crossed out the first one having wasted 10 minutes.

    D Candidate got carried away. Put all she knew about the subject. Got good mark for the question, but only completed half the number of questions required, and failed the exam.

7. Suppose in an exam you have 3 hours to do 5 questions. Why is it very important to allow the same time for each question, rather than letting the 'best two' eat up most of the time?

    A Because if I only do three questions as a result of spending too long on the first two, my maximum mark would only be 60%.

    B Because the first few marks on any question are much easier to get than the last few – so it's easier to get the first 8 marks on the last question than it is to get the last 2 marks on the first.

    C Because I can always go back and make some additions later to may first 2 questions (my last one or two won't take so long, because I'll usually know less about them).

    D Because if I spend too long on a question I'm good at, the chances are that I'm putting in extra material that isn't earning me any extra marks.

8. Suppose you decide to write your answers in one colour, and underline headings and important words in another colour so that

they stand out more clearly. Which of the following combinations is best? (You can swap black for blue if you prefer).

A Writing in green ink, headings underlined in red ink.
B Writing in black ink, headings underlined in red ink.
C Writing in black ink, headings underlined in green ink.
D Writing in green ink, headings underlined in black ink.

9. It's worth leaving some spare time for the end of an exam. For a 3-hour exam, I'd say about 20 minutes should be saved for the end. Below is a list of things you can do in those 20 minutes. Which do you think will earn you the most marks?

A Finish off any questions that are still incomplete.
B Read through every word you have written, making additions and corrections as you go.
C Tidy up your paper, making it easier for the examiner to find his way around it.
D Had enough! Go out and have a cup of coffee.

10. Have we made you feel better about exams in this course? Which statement applies best to you?

A I was always scared stiff of exams, and I still am.
B I used to be scared stiff of exams, but I feel much happier about them now, knowing how to tackle them in a logical way.
C I never used to worry about exams, but I feel more worried about them now.
D I've never been worried by exams, I just do the best I can.

APPENDIX 2: FURTHER READING

If you want to read more on the topics we have covered, these books will be useful to you.

Study

Maddox, Harry. *How to study.* Pan Books, London, rev. edn. 1967.
Pauk, W. *How to study in college.* Houghton Mifflin, Boston, 1974.
Rowntree, Derek. *Learn how to study.* Macdonald, London, rev. edn. 1976 (programmed for individual study, with activities).

Memory

Higbee, K. L. *Your memory: how it works and how to improve it.* Prentice Hall, New Jersey, 1977.

Reading

de Leeuw, Manya Eric. *Read better, read faster.* Penguin, London, 1965.
Lloyd, Susan M. (ed). *Roget's thesaurus.* Longman, Harlow, 1982.
Mares, C. *Efficient reading.* Hodder & Stoughton, London, 1976.

Note-taking

Buzan, Tony. *Use your head.* BBC Publications, London, 1974.

Essay Writing

Gowers, Sir Ernest. *The complete plain words.* Penguin, London, 1962.
Jones, Rhodri. *A new English course.* Heinemann & NEC, Cambridge, 1975.
Lewis, Roger. *How to write essays.* NEC, Cambridge, revised edition 1984. (Available only from NEC.)
Lister, T. A. *Writing for everyone.* NEC, Cambridge, 1973. (Available only from NEC.)
Marland, M. & Thompson, D. *English for the individual.* Heinemann, London, 1964 (programmed for individual study).

SIGNING OFF

We hope you found this course interesting and useful. Remember that to get the most out of it, and out of your studies, you must try and apply its principles at every opportunity. Making good study habits is a slow job and requires perseverance. If this course has shown you what to do and if it encourages you to go on and do it, it has achieved its aim.

Richard Freeman
Carol Harman